PAT
COWDEL

The Hardest Game

HARRY CARPENTER

The Hardest Game

Photographs by Chris Moyse

BRITISH BROADCASTING CORPORATION

Published by the British Broadcasting Corporation,
35 Marylebone High Street, London W1M 4AA

ISBN 0 563 17945 7

First published 1981

Made by Lennard Books,
The Old School,
Wheathampstead, Herts AL4 8AN
Editor Michael Leitch
Designed by David Pocknell's Company Limited
Design Assistant Barry Lowenhoff
Production Reynolds Clark Associates Limited
Printed and bound in Spain by
Novograph SA, Madrid
Dep. Legal M 26082/1981

Photographs for Chapter Nine
supplied by Gilbert Odd

CONTENTS

CHAPTER ONE

THE MOMENT OF TRIUMPH

At the centre of a big arena, 400 square feet of roped canvas, bathed in light, where a man's life is changed forever in one hour, or one minute, or just 10 seconds.

GT BRITAIN
GT BRITAIN

White light beats down on a ring besieged by people. The ring won't hold any more, but more are fighting to get in and policemen struggle to hold them out. One man more hysterical than the rest tries to hurl himself into the ring off the Press bench. His foot squashes hard down on the keys of a typewriter. A reporter's hand happens to be there at the time. The world is full of noisy, trampling, sweating, cheering, swearing, happy, angry people. The Big Fight is over. The MC fishes for his microphone in a sea of feet: 'My Lords, ladies and gentlemen. . . .'

The scene freezes like a TV action replay and the mob collects itself for one final orgy of noise. 'The Winner. . . !' The frame unfreezes and the mob picks up where it left off, shoving, shouting, scrambling, tearing its way to be near . . . 'The Winner!' The world has a new champion and somewhere in that heaving mass he is being hugged, pummelled, slapped, kissed, pushed, pulled, being handled, in fact, with every response but dignity. For the time being, dignity is out.

Boxers react in numerous ways to their Moment of Triumph. Most jump two feet off the floor, brandishing their fists. Some fall into their managers' arms in a loving embrace. Some kiss their trainers, others look for wives or girl-friends. Some sink to their knees, others cross themselves. None that I remember ever shrugged his shoulders, muttered 'That's it, then,' and climbed out of the

The Moment of Triumph: for Lotte Mwale, of Zambia, at Wembley, where his arm is raised by referee Harry Gibbs. Mwale, light-heavyweight champion of the Commonwealth, has just outpointed Jesse Burnett in an eliminator for the world title. Nine months later, in San Diego, Mwale's bid for the title ended disastrously, when Matthew Saad Muhammad beat him in four rounds.

ring. Why should he? Only a handful of special men from the entire population of the world experience boxing's Moment of Triumph. 'The Winner! . . . World Champion!' The Moment, when it comes, is a whirling kaleidoscope, a frenzy of jubilation in a ridiculously confined space. It is utterly unlike any other comparable Moment in sport.

The new champion is reluctant to leave the ring. His Moment must be savoured, stretched, preserved. If only he could hold on to it for ever, on this tiny stage, 20ft x 20ft, where for the last hour he has concentrated everything he's ever learned about boxing, 10 years of toil, into one great effort to beat the other man. Now victory has changed his life for good.

At one time the Moment of Triumph was rarely enjoyed by Britain's boxers. Before World War II our men seldom took part in world-title fights and hardly ever won them. In the 1930s, we produced only four world champions. Three of these were flyweights, the 112-lb division where we had traditional strength. They were Jackie Brown, Benny Lynch and Peter Kane. Our only other world champion in those 10 years was Jack Kid Berg at junior-welter (140lb), a division almost totally confined to the United States, although Berg won his title in London. Professional boxing in the 1930s was dominated by the USA who had most of the world champions and controlled the sport. It continued to be so for some time after the war until air travel (you could not fly to the States before the war) opened up the game. With easier international exchange, America's grip was broken and today she herself struggles to make an impression on world boxing, except at the heavier weights, where she still rules.

The face of world professional boxing has changed dramatically in the last 25 years. At one time there were only eight traditional weights and, generally speaking, just one recognized champion at each weight. We all knew who he was. Not so today. As I write, there are 15 weight divisions, starting from light-flyweight (108lb), and, because the sport has opposing governing bodies, the World Boxing Association and the World Boxing Council, two champions at each weight . . . well, almost. At the beginning of 1981 there were 28 'world' champions!

The only reason there were not 30 was that the WBA had not got around to declaring a super-fly (115lb) champion, while at middleweight Marvin Hagler of the USA was recognized by both camps. Small wonder that even the expert today finds it impossible to name all the champions. From being badly under-organized, professional boxing today is madly over-organized, with the unhappy result that most 'world' champions are really only half-champions. They know – and we know – there is one other man in the world they have not met

Sid Nathan, one of Britain's smaller referees, barely tops John Feeney, the Hartlepool bantamweight. Feeney has just beaten Neil McLaughlin of Ireland inside three rounds. But, four months later, in his next fight in this same Wembley ring, Feeney was despondent when he failed to beat Johnny Owen, of Wales, for the British and Commonwealth titles.

Spectacular triumph, for Welshman Colin Jones at the Royal Albert Hall. The American Richard House is on the floor. Jones, British welter-weight champion, has put him there with one right hand. Mike Jacobs, the referee, having counted 'ten', bends solicitously over the stricken American. Jones has won in 2min 27sec.

and he is the man who might beat them.

However, from this post-war expansion and our more sophisticated knowledge of preparing boxers and steering them to title fights has come a remarkable bonus of success. The man who started it all was the hugely popular Freddie Mills, no very skilful boxer but a game and colourful fighter who, in 1948, won the world light-heavyweight crown from the American Gus Lesnevitch. When Randolph Turpin surpassed even Mills's efforts and took the middleweight title from the legendary Sugar Ray Robinson in 1951, British boxing assumed a world importance it had not enjoyed since the early days of the century. It has never looked back and in recent years we have relished the successes of Walter McGowan, Terry Downes, Howard Winstone, Ken Buchanan, John Stracey and John Conteh.

In 1980 came the finest year of all: three world champions for Britain at the same time – Jim Watt, Maurice Hope, Alan Minter, triumph on a scale we could not have dared to visualize 20 years earlier. And yet . . . for every winner, there must be a loser, and for every world champion, hundreds, thousands, of boxers who never make it. Most never escape the humdrum six- and eight-round fights, the realistic core of the sport. These men dream about, but never experience, the Moment of Triumph. Boxing is truly The Hardest Game.

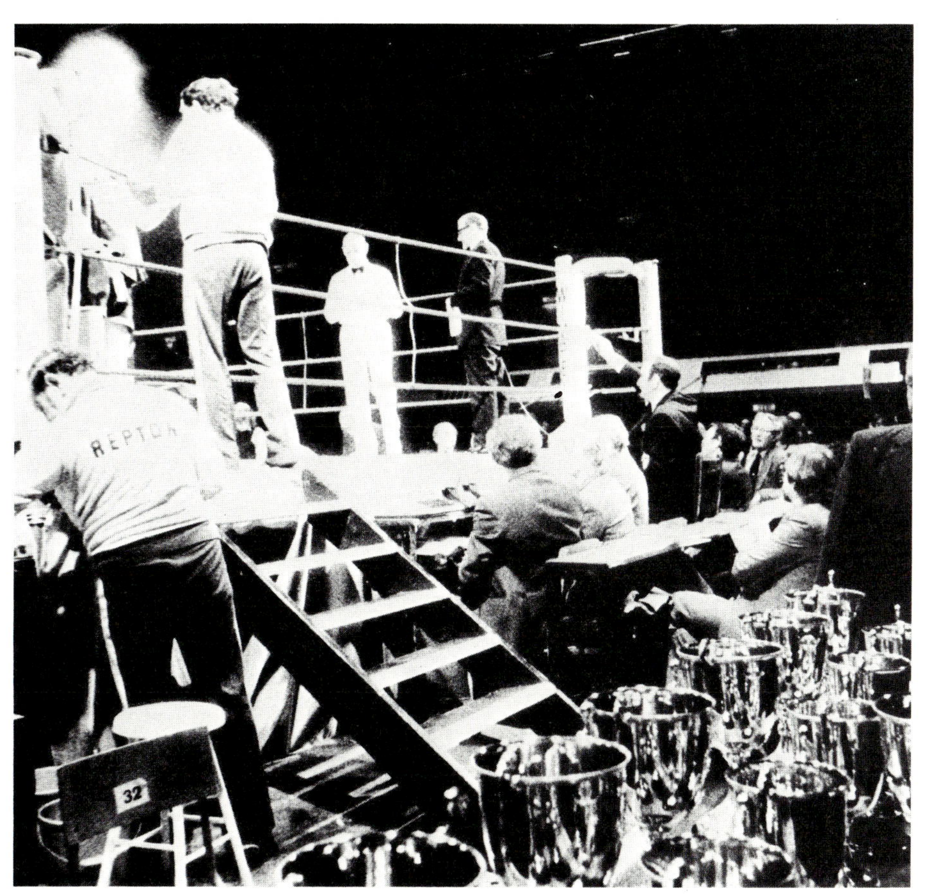

CHAPTER TWO
STARTING OUT

The silverware—and the steps to where it's won. For Britain's amateur boxers, the big night of the year comes at Wembley in the ABA Finals. Gleaming prizes await the winners. Years of effort lie between these trophies and the boy starting out.

Muhammad Ali started when he was 12 and beat Sonny Liston for the world heavyweight title when he had just turned 22. Ten years to reach the top is about average. Ali weighed 112lb when he walked into a boxing gym for the first time. A Kentucky cop gave him his first lesson. Most boys in Britain begin to box seriously round about 11 or 12. That is the age when schools and clubs first organize them into national competition. But they may begin much earlier. Brian London, former British heavyweight champion, told me he threw his first punches when his father, who had held the same title, got down on his knees on the living-room floor and showed him how to shape up. Brian was three or four at the time. Boxing often runs in families. Henry Cooper's grandfather fought bareknuckle or with gloves. He didn't care which. A boy with a relative who boxed is bound to hear about it and the spark is struck. Or he is taken to a club by schoolmates who box, and starts from there. The armed forces firmly encourage boxing but, since the demise of National Service, no longer shine at it. The public schools, former strongholds of the sport, no longer regard it as an acceptable sporting discipline, with a few exceptions. University boxing is sparse and not of high quality.

Without conducting a mass social survey it is safe to say that the average British boxer springs from what is still called the working class and has most chance of succeeding if he lives in a big city where amateur clubs are accessible and good-class coaching available. Almost every professional champion, British or otherwise, began as an amateur. Ken Buchanan, Jim Watt, John Stracey, Maurice Hope, John Conteh, Alan Minter and Henry Cooper all started at school or club level, and all of them lived in or near a major city.

A boy's first experience of boxing is likely to be in a tiny, dimly-lit, poorly-heated gymnasium with a minimum of equipment and hardly any staff. Most amateur clubs are woefully short of funds and held together by one or two men with great dollops of enthusiasm. The boy will be in the hands of the club trainer, almost certainly a former boxer, and tested in the privacy of the gym against boys of his age, weight and experience. If he shows natural ability he may be allowed to proceed to boxing in public at carefully regulated shows under the control of the Amateur Boxing Association, to which all schools, clubs, officials and boxers must be affiliated. I have never had any doubt about the social benefits of amateur boxing at this level. For a start, and to put it crudely, it takes them off the streets. The Schools' Boxing Association and the National Association of Boys' Clubs, both of whom run their own championships, seem to me to stand for what is best in sport: disciplined youngsters excelling at their chosen pastime, able perhaps to catch a glimpse of an exciting future, and demon-

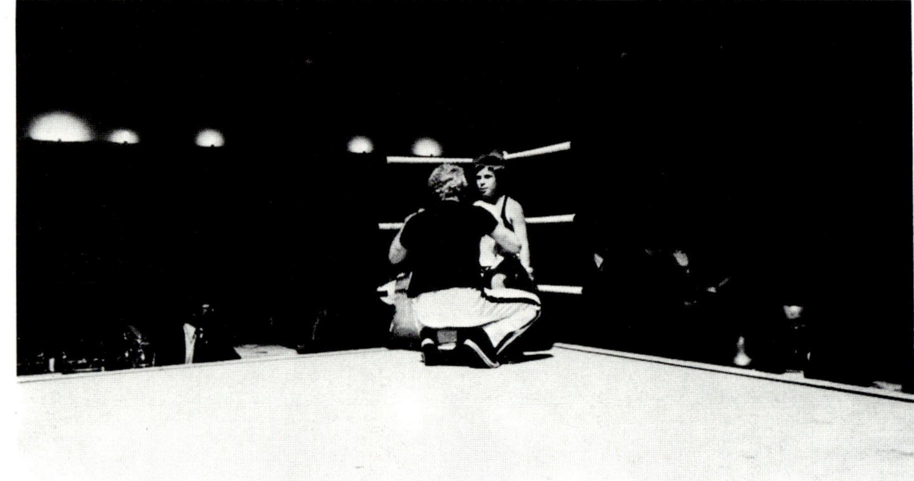

Big ring, small boy . . . how it looks to a young kid at his first amateur show. Once, he would have boxed in his local town hall or the working men's club. Today, he's more likely to be part of a dinner-boxing show, perhaps in a hotel, with dinner-jacketed spectators and drinks on the ringside tables.

strating that in life it is possible to give a knock and take one without losing your temper. End of sermon.

Amazingly, each year well over 6,000 boys are entered for the Schools' Championships. When you remember that throughout Britain there are only 600 or 700 professional boxers, it is obvious that somewhere between school and leaving it, there

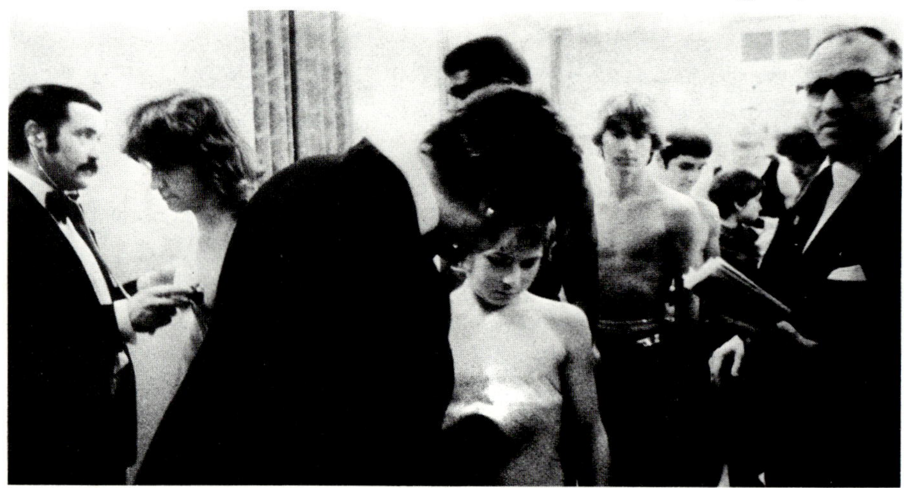

Breathe in . . . the medical officers for the show have left their table at the ringside, hence the dinner-jackets.

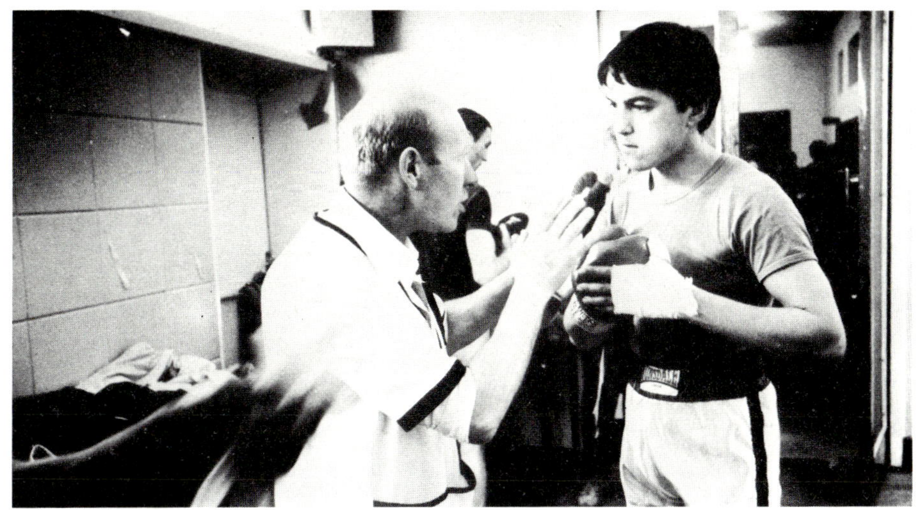

Last-minute coaching . . . a bit late for that now. The strips of adhesive tape on the wall are used to hold the bandages in place on the hands.

is a massive drop-out from boxing. It comes, of course, when the boy has to earn a living. At this point, discos appeal more than discipline, and girls have more attraction for teenage hands than gloves. Boxing for most boys never extends beyond a small local show: the changing-room is the size of a small cupboard, and there may not even be a shower.

The patrons . . . more and more shows, amateur and professional, are staged like this. Best bib-and-tucker, a fair nosh, plenty to drink, a fat cigar, blood-and-thumps for afters. Not the traditional image of amateur boxing. The diehards hate it, but simple economics have brought it about.

Right
Without selfless servants like him, amateur boxing would perish. Most will never send a boy to Wembley for the big night. They still hope.
Far right
The moment any boxer dreads . . . down and hurt.

The referee orders your opponent to a neutral corner. He's OK. Where am I? What am I doing?

Someone's counting at me. He thinks I'm not listening, so he's doing it on his fingers as well.

Far left
Ten! I know, I know. You don't have to show me. I've blown it.
Left
The winner . . . who cares about a cut under the eye? Another trophy for the sideboard.

But if the boy really is good enough, he moves from Schools' and NABC Championships to the ABA Junior Championships, and so into the seniors at 17, and the immensely demanding ABA Championships themselves through district, regional

This is it . . . the ambition of every amateur's life. The annual ABA Finals, the national championships, at Wembley on the first Friday in May. Out there, in the dark, 10,000 excited people. Seated ringside, the Press. Perched above them, one of the three judges. On his left, BBC-TV's ringside camera and, left again, the TV commentator, wearing headphones and looking into his monitor screen. Flooded by light, the principals: the boxers and the referee, plus a cornerman slow to leave the ring.

and inter-zone competitions, and on to the televised National Finals, held on the first Friday in May at Wembley Arena before 10,000 people. At this level the young boxer's world widens and offers the tempting chance of globetrotting with English,

Right
The pre-Final pose, awkwardly self-conscious: Welsh heavy-weight Rudi Pika, whose father came from Estonia, squares up, southpaw-style. Rudi got to Wembley two years running, but didn't win a Final. Now he fights for money.
Far right
Scottish light-welter John McAllister waits to box his final. He's tense. Two other Scots have already lost. He's Scotland's last hope. But Tony Willis of England beat him. Scotland's amateur boxing is no longer the force it was.

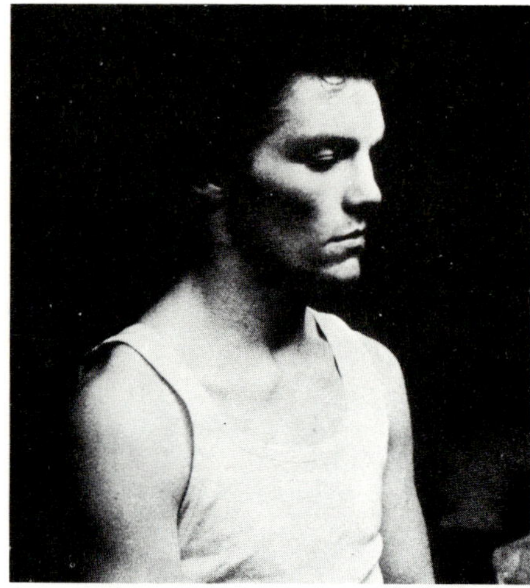

Before the action starts, bureaucracy behind the scenes. Each boxer's medical book is checked by an ABA official.

Irish, Scottish or Welsh teams, perhaps a place in the European Championships against the mighty Russians and Poles, and ultimately – given only to a few – a trip to the Olympic Games, a medal perhaps, even gold.

Britain's collection of gold from nine Olympic Games held since 1948 is meagre. Only three men have won: Terry Spinks (fly) and Dick McTaggart (light) in Melbourne, 1956, and Chris Finnegan (middle) in Mexico, 1968. The scarcity of

Brian Pollard will referee some of the Finals. His badge, issued by AIBA, the international governing body of amateur boxing, signifies that Pollard is qualified to judge and referee at all levels of the sport, including the Olympic Games.

Into the ring and just three rounds away from being Britain's champion at light-flyweight (7½ stone). Lancashire's John Lyon, from St Helen's, is famous enough to merit a dressing-gown with his name on. He follows referee Pollard into the ring. Opponent Terry Barker, from London's famous Repton club in Bethnal Green, is already there. So is MC George Parker, one-time warrant officer in the RAF.

gold tells two stories: the intense difficulty of being the best in a world teeming with amateur boxers (250,000 in the Soviet Union alone), but, more importantly, the near impossibility today of winning Olympic fame from a system which is still as strictly amateur in Britain as it was when the ABA was founded over 100 years ago.

Elsewhere, notably in Eastern Europe and Cuba, the system is blatantly semi-professional. Boxers, State-aided, have 'jobs' which enable them to be full-time boxers. A British amateur must earn his livelihood, perhaps support a family, fit his training into his spare time and rely on a benevolent employer giving him time off to travel to championships or tour with the national team. Given that

Jimmy Price, from Liverpool, hammers away at Bristol's Nick Wilshire in the light-middleweight (11st 2lb) final. Bottom left, Bill Martin, of the Press Association. He's been reporting boxing, amateur and pro, for 30 years.

Heavyweight Pika between rounds.

startling difference between the systems, it is a minor miracle that our boxers come home from Olympic or European Championships with medals at all. But they do.

Their homes are choc-à-bloc with prizes. Show me a top-class amateur and I will show you a house stuffed full of plaques, cups and trophies of every shape and size, an Aladdin's cave of electric blankets, tea-kettles, toasters and cutlery. By the time a good amateur is 18, there is nothing he hasn't won, except MONEY. No wonder he begins to think about getting paid for what he does so well. He may look for a professional manager. The chances are, he won't have to. The manager will be looking for him.

The light-flyweights have finished their three rounds. Pollard collects the judges' score-cards and hands them in for scrutiny. Terry Barker marks time, trying to relax, but can't until he knows the result.

He knows now . . . all three judges vote for 17-year-old Barker, who jumps for joy. For loser Lyon, the season's effort has come to nothing. If you lose the big one, you've lost the lot. But next year Lyon was back, as a winner.

In the first few heady minutes as champion, Terry Barker celebrates . . . with mineral water. But somebody's already been at the champagne, by the look of that other bottle.

Another bottle of bubbly, and a cup to pour it in, belonging to Tony Willis, the new ABA light-welterweight champion. Less than three months later, Willis returned home to Liverpool from Moscow with an Olympic bronze medal. He was Britain's only boxing medal-winner there.

Left
Tony Burns, Barker's coach, takes his other Repton finalist, lightweight Tony Bowden, to the presentation from the Duke of Fife. But Bowden's cup is the runner-up's. George Gilbody, Britain's Olympic boxing captain, has outpointed him. The Duke is vice-patron of the ABA. The Patron? Prince Philip.

Another winner, although you'd hardly guess it from the faces: heavyweight Frank Bruno, from Wandsworth. On the right, his mate, Frankie Lucas, who once boxed for the same club as Bruno, Croydon's Sir Philip Game ABC. Lucas won two ABA titles in the early 1970s, then turned pro. Bruno also tried to go professional, but failed the British Boxing Board's eyesight test.

CHAPTER THREE
THE CHANGEOVER

For John Dorey, just turning professional, this is a new experience. Previously his amateur club at Eltham provided most of the gear. Now he must buy all his own kit. John reached the London ABA featherweight semi-finals in 1980.

The symbolic gesture for a boy going pro is shedding his amateur singlet. Now he boxes bare from the waist up. The world is a much tougher place. Not only does he hope to make a living punching with his fists. Others now rely on *him* to make a living for *them*. The manager, for example, gets 25 per cent of his purse-money. The gym, which back at the amateur club was full of friends, is now an alien place packed with strangers. If it is a fashionable camp, some of those training around him may have familiar faces and household names: but they are seasoned pros. He is the raw novice, no matter how respected he was in the amateur ranks.

The full set of gear for a pro boxer. Clockwise from top left: skipping-rope; tracksuit top and running socks; running shoes; adhesive tape (for hands) and boxing trunks; dressing-gown; tracksuit trousers; boxing boots and fight socks; foul-proof cup; training T-shirts; training shorts and weight-reducing sweatsuit. Centre: sparring mitts; boxing gloves; ball-punching gloves. Total cost: £200 approx.

For the first time in his life he may have opened a bank account. There could even be a bit put away. The manager, if he's adept at finding good 'spots' on big promotions for his fighters, may have slipped him a few quid 'just for starters'. The business of 'buying' amateurs is frowned upon, but it happens. Competition for new talent is fierce. The danger is apparent. The manager, having made his 'investment', is conscious that he must get it back before he starts to make a profit. The temptation comes to push the boy too hard, too quickly, into fights which pay more but may be too difficult for him at that stage of his career.

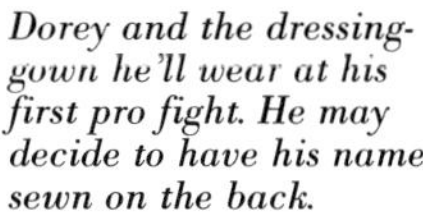

Dorey and the dressing-gown he'll wear at his first pro fight. He may decide to have his name sewn on the back.

Jimmy Flint was once an ABA Junior champion. Now he's a veteran pro who has boxed for a British title. At 28, Flint knows his way round the shop that sells boxing gear. He's been in and out for years, ever since he turned pro in 1973.

The late Jim Wicks, one of Britain's most successful managers (he looked after Henry Cooper, and Henry has no complaints) always swore he had never paid an amateur to turn pro with him. Jim had such a reputation for steering his men capably to the top, he had no need to lure them with immediate cash offers. Class amateurs gravitated towards Wicks. A manager's reputation matters more than the size of the wad in his pocket.

Not all top-class amateurs elect to go pro. Nicky Gargano, of England, won the ABA welter championship three years running, from 1954–56, won the Commonwealth (then the Empire) Games gold medal in 1954, a European gold in 1955, and Olympic bronze in Melbourne, 1956. He retired shortly afterwards, never tempted to be a pro. Today he's a successful London publican, with no regrets. Nicky, a southpaw, was as expert a boxer as I have seen. He could overcome anyone's style; what you might call a boxer's boxer. But I think he knew in his heart that the pro game calls for something more lurid. He would never have been what managers and promoters call a 'crowd-pleaser'. Crowd-pleasers earn good money. They can also get hurt. Crowd-pleasers must take a few, as well as give them.

Dick McTaggart, of Scotland, another southpaw, a contemporary of Nicky, was even more successful, winning everything from RAF to Olympic

championships. Dick, a member of a famous Dundee boxing family, was a TV favourite of the 1950s and '60s. He won five ABA titles, Empire Games gold, European gold, Olympic gold and bronze!
But he would not be tempted to turn professional. Dick was an extraordinary ring artist. He never seemed to exert himself. He had a built-in ability to judge just how much work was needed to steal a decision. He was the epitome of the canny Scot, canny enough to turn a deaf 'un to the blatant cries of the money men. I remember calling on him in a Dundee tenement when he was at the height of his fame. He'd just married and had a job which wasn't bringing in much. But he'd shut the door on a Scottish manager who had dumped a gigantic bundle of banknotes on the kitchen table with the words: 'They're all for you, if you turn pro with me.' Dick knew only too well that there is a world of difference between outsmarting an amateur over three rounds and having to do it against a pro over six, eight or ten.

That is the physical change the new professional notices. No more three-rounders. The very least in pro boxing is four. A good amateur is more likely to start over six, or even eight. It calls for a new approach. Stamina can be squandered recklessly over three rounds. It must be spread carefully over eight. A hard, strong, wild-punching opponent, easily outfoxed for nine minutes, is a different animal over 24 minutes.

The most financially successful changeover in Britain in recent years was made by heavyweight Billy Walker, who had all the attributes to appeal to promoters: big, handsome, hard-hitting, exciting to watch, a natural for the pro ranks, a point which did not escape that wily old promoter Harry Levene, who signed him up for his first three fights at the unprecedented fee of £10,000. Walker was riotously successful at the box-office from 1962 – 69. But the very quality which ensured that – an abandoned, free-swinging style as reckless as it was exciting – meant he was never good enough to win a title. It didn't seem to matter.

Pete Rademacher, of the USA, who was Olympic heavyweight champion in 1956, made the most astounding transition of all. In August 1957, in Seattle, in his first professional fight, he challenged Floyd Patterson for the world heavyweight title. Although he had Patterson down in the second round, Rademacher was counted out in the sixth, after seven knockdowns, a cynical and irresponsible piece of matchmaking with nothing more to recommend it than an eye for the quick buck. Rademacher boxed for five years as a pro, but never won an important fight.

The hard fact of life for most professionals in Britain – or anywhere, for that matter – is that they will never be successful enough to earn a living

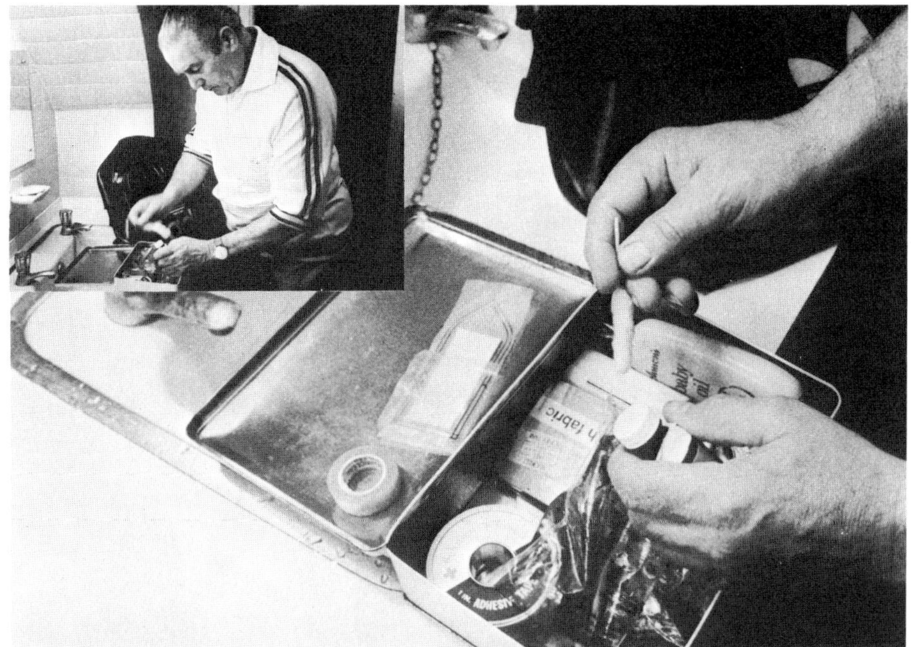

The cut-man's kit: the tin-box of medicaments taken into the corner on fight-night. It contains swabsticks, adhesive tape, sticking plasters, antiseptic gauze, cotton-wool, baby-oil and the vital bottle of weak adrenalin, the only coagulant permitted under Boxing Board rules for treating cuts around the eyes. The solution strength is laid down: one part adrenalin to 1,000 parts water.
Inset
Britain's top cut-man: Danny Holland. For years, Danny worked with Henry Cooper, a frequent caller on his expertise.

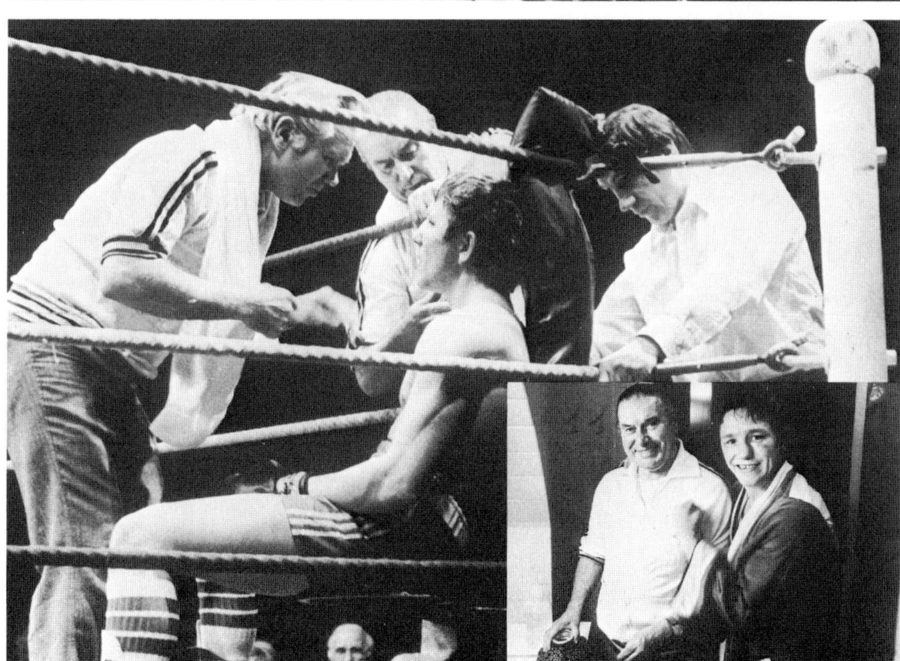

Fight-night at the Albert Hall; Danny is there in case Dave Boy Green (and manager Andy Smith) need him.
Inset
On this night Danny's skills were almost unused. Green, the winner, escapes uncut. But the ice-bag Danny is holding helped reduce the swelling under Dave's left eye.

solely as a boxer. They have to find another job. They will also be expected to go among their friends and flog tickets for their fights. A fighter must try to sell enough tickets to cover his purse money. It's not enough just to get up there and box.

Nothing daunted, the new pro can't wait to buy his gear: jazzy satin trunks, soft leather boots, smart socks, sequinned robe with his name on, even if he does have to borrow the money to pay for it all. If he was well publicized as an amateur, he might find himself making his professional début at Wembley or the Albert Hall, but it will probably be in the first fight of the night, when half the crowd are still parking their cars. Never mind. He's on his way. Optimism is rife. He's a pro at last. Earning a few quid. Look out, world, here I come!

Let's hope he wins. A boxer called Dave Dunn, of Manchester, turned professional in 1973, and lost both his fights that year. In 1974 he lost twice more. He had a long rest, tried again in 1977, and lost. In 1978 he had three fights and lost them all. Another rest. He came back in 1980 and lost twice more. Then, in January 1981, he made it at last: his first professional win after more than seven years. Oddly enough, the man he beat was having *his* first pro fight.

CHAPTER FOUR

THE WORLD OF PROFESSIONALISM

Jesse Burnett in his Wembley dressing-room, the night of his fight against Lotte Mwale. Because Burnett is American and unused to British rules, referee Harry Gibbs has come to explain them. Board inspector Harry Vines is also going over the formalities with manager Jesse Reid, partly hidden by Burnett.

The curious, close-knit world of big-time pro boxing: weighing-in for an important fight. The promoters have hired the Dominion Cinema, Tottenham Court Road, for the ceremony. On the scales, tipping them at 12st 6lb, Lotte Mwale, of Zambia, the Commonwealth light-heavyweight champion, who's been brought to Europe as a world-title hope. Checking the weight, British Boxing Board of Control inspector Harry Vines. Carefully watching, over Vines's right shoulder, Ray Clarke, the Board's general secretary. Watching, even more carefully, over Vines's other shoulder, Mickey Duff, the most influential man in British boxing. Duff is not only co-promoting the show, he's co-manager of Mwale as well. Just in front of the man in the trilby hat is George Francis, Mwale's trainer. Behind Duff, to the left, Jesse Reid, American manager of Mwale's opponent, Jesse Burnett, who's already weighed in, half a pound heavier, and gone. The rest are other managers, other trainers, reporters, photographers, one or two punters who've bought tickets for the fight, and some lookers-on who've just walked in from the street to brighten up an otherwise dull lunch-hour.

Cartoonists draw fight promoters as portly gentlemen, flashily dressed, with torpedo cigars jammed permanently in their mouths . . . they draw bookmakers in precisely the same way, which is shrewd. Many a promoter has been a bookie, the late Jack Solomons for one. Solomons, I suppose, came as near the cartoon image of a promoter as anyone. He was certainly portly, his suits were spectacular, and the big cigar was his trademark. But there is a limit with fight promoters. Solomons made a packet over the years, but never invested any of it in flashy offices. Harry Levene, today's leading London promoter, also sports a cigar at the ringside, because he probably feels he has to, and would be totally downcast if you imagined he had paid less than £500 for any one of his innumerable perfect suits. And yet, if you go to see Harry in his Soho office, you

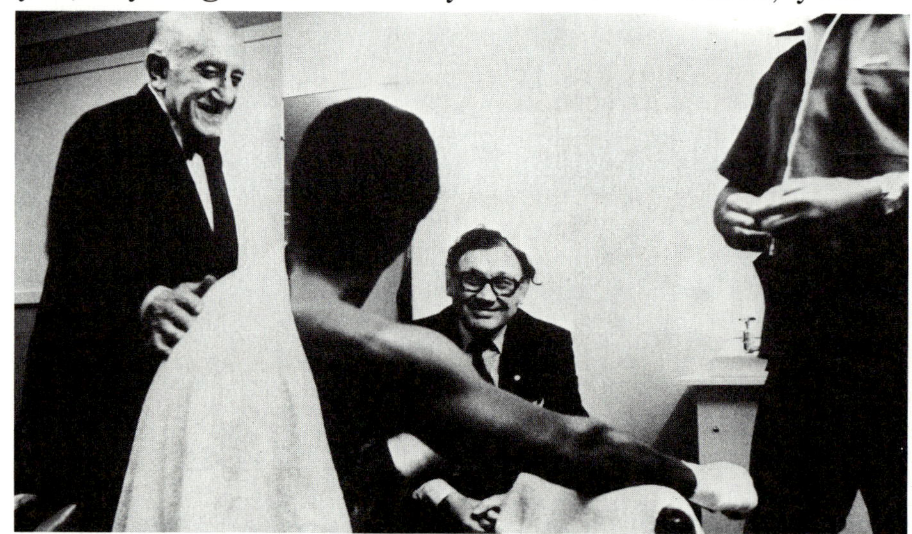

Duff's co-promoter, Harry Levene, has come to chat with the American he's invested in. Levene, who never reveals his age ('I'm 39, like Jack Benny') is Britain's senior promoter. He's been closely associated with the game since before World War I. London-born, Levene managed fighters in the States while still in his teens. Jock McAvoy and Dave Crowley, two of Britain's best champions between the wars, were his. So was Larry Gains, the great Canadian heavyweight.

find him up a narrow flight of dingy stairs, perched above a tobacconist and a tailor. Solomons had a gym and a suite of offices on the second floor over a billiard hall in Great Windmill Street, opposite the Windmill Theatre ('We Never Clothed'). Getting to it was an obstacle course, threading your way past the dustbins on the landing.

Behind the scenes, professional boxing has always been seedy, and endlessly fascinating. You may think Damon Runyon was exaggerating, but he wasn't. Although today boxing in Britain has abandoned the squalid local halls where it used to thrive and has moved into the flash wining-and-dining clubs of big hotels up and down the country, promoters still operate from cramped offices in mean streets. You must enter the domain of the closed-circuit TV executive if you hanker after

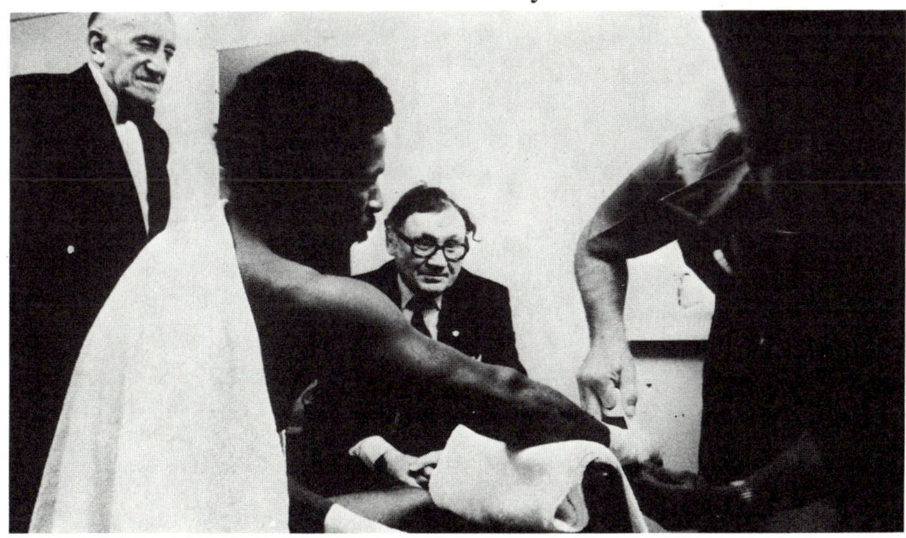

Bandages, up to 18 feet of them on either hand, have been wound round Burnett's fists. Now zinc oxide sticky tape, 11 feet of it, is added, to form a compact protective casing over all knuckles. Bespectacled Ron Pudney, former classy middleweight from Croydon, now a steward for the Board of Control, supervises the bandaging.

glass-topped desks, louvre-draped windows and leather armchairs.

In Britain, professional boxing is a tight-knit, intimate world of 600 or so professional boxers who are looked after by about as many people again. They include promoters, matchmakers (they advise promoters on who should fight whom), managers, agents, trainers, seconds, doctors, MCs, referees, timekeepers and whips (the chaps who hustle boxers in and out of the ring on fight nights).

Every one of these people (other than the doctor) is licensed by, and answerable to, the British Boxing Board of Control, sole governing body of the professional sport in this country. It has existed since 1929. Its headquarters is just round the back of the London Palladium near Oxford Circus, where a small paid staff operates under the benevolent

Pudney scrawls his signature across the finished taping, to OK the bandaging and ensure it's not tampered with.

guidance of the stewards, unpaid and non-financially interested officials who formulate rules and sit in judgment on those who break them. From this London HQ, the Board controls boxing nationwide through its Area Councils and representative stewards. This tried and proven system of government frequently comes in for criticism from its licence holders, but has successfully held together the sport in Britain for more than half a century. Given the free-wheeling, undercover, sharp-edged, furiously competitive, money-conscious nature of the professional game, the Board's achievements are little short of miraculous. The Board gives British boxing the moral lead and respectability without which it would quickly founder.

It exists financially – certainly not grandly – on the licence fees it demands from its members,

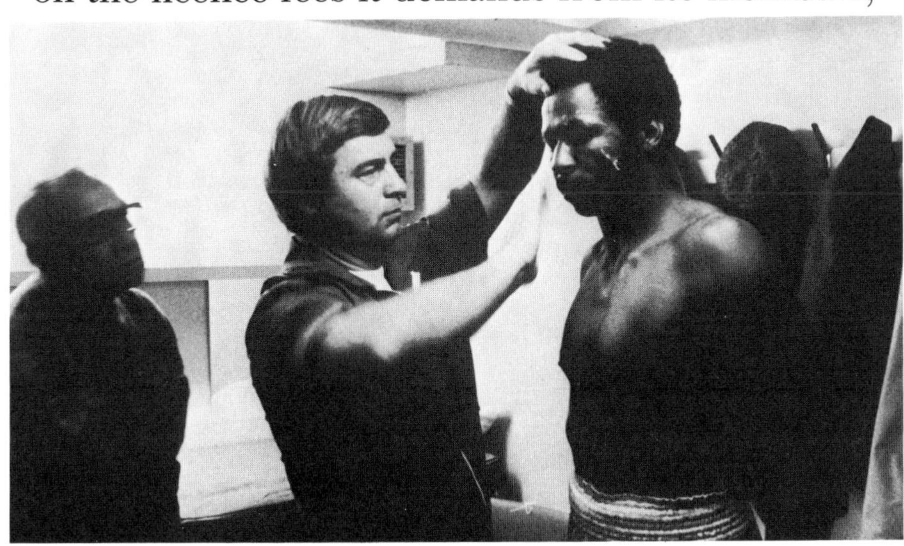

As fight-time approaches, manager Reid smears grease over Burnett's ring-worn face. In theory, Mwale's gloves—or head—will slide over the grease, minimizing the danger of cuts. But some trainers believe grease softens the skin too much, making cuts more likely.

Burnett, in his corner, receives the final finger-wagging talking-to from his manager. Twelve rounds later, Burnett lost the decision. But many in the Wembley crowd booed Harry Gibbs's scoring. Burnett returned to the States and in his next fight beat former world champion, Victor Galindez.
Inset
In the other dressing-room, Mwale waits with Duff, the man who's got him this fight and who will help him get a world title fight, if he wins this one.

plus its percentage of boxers' purses and promoters' takings. No British championship can be staged without Board sanction and it must nominate or approve all challengers. The abiding, shining quality is the impartial integrity of its stewards. The Board's constitution clearly owes something to the way horseracing is administered, not surprising when you realize how closely Lord Lonsdale, that expansive patron of the Turf, was associated with boxing in its earlier days. The Board, like the Jockey Club, relied heavily on retired military gentlemen for its stewards at the start. Not a bad policy. Today the Board has a wholesome respect for tradition, the backbone of sport, and its offices are a small treasurehouse of sacred objects – ancient belts and historic paintings.

Perhaps its most romantic link with boxing's past is the continued awarding of the Lonsdale Belt to British champions. Three British title wins at the same weight entitle a champion to retain the Belt. Like so many of these hallowed traditions, the Lonsdale Belt, far from being a romantic inspiration of Lord Lonsdale, had its foundation in something far more practical.

It goes back to the days of the National Sporting Club in Covent Garden around the turn of the century. The Club, with good reason, considered itself the governing body of the sport at that time, but as years went by its authority was challenged.

In 1909 the inaugural Belt was presented to Freddie Welsh, the lightweight champion. The point was then made that only the holder of the Lonsdale Belt would be recognized as the official champion of Britain. Furthermore, the Belt could only be fought for at the National Sporting Club! This ingenious piece of administration maintained the NSC in a

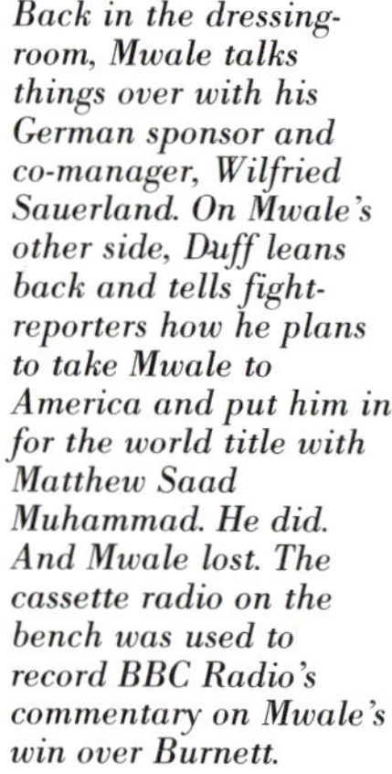

Back in the dressing-room, Mwale talks things over with his German sponsor and co-manager, Wilfried Sauerland. On Mwale's other side, Duff leans back and tells fight-reporters how he plans to take Mwale to America and put him in for the world title with Matthew Saad Muhammad. He did. And Mwale lost. The cassette radio on the bench was used to record BBC Radio's commentary on Mwale's win over Burnett.

position of power for a few more years. But eventually the Club crumbled away and for a time the sport floundered unmanageably, until the British Boxing Board of Control was founded in 1929.

The Lonsdale Belt, symbol of control in British boxing, is still with us. Once upon a time, it was made of solid gold. Indeed, Henry Cooper has one such belt among the three he won. But today, a sign of our devalued times, it is silver-gilt. But then, so is an Olympic 'gold' medal.

CHAPTER FIVE
A FIGHTER'S LIFE

Roadwork: the hardest part of training, but essential. Miles of running, in all weathers, usually done at crack of dawn, before petrol fumes pollute the air. A lonely discipline, to put strength in legs and lungs. Success in a long, difficult fight may well depend on how conscientious the roadwork has been.

Three minutes. The duration of a round of boxing. A tiny fraction of time that dominates every fighter's thinking. Tiny, yes, in the context of a whole day. But in the ring, on fight night, three minutes is forever, with three more coming up, and another three after that . . . and all the while an opponent hammering at you. If you break a fight down to its crudest terms, it becomes a starkly simple problem: how to survive three minutes under another man's onslaught. Which is why a fighter's mind must work to the rigid discipline of three minutes.

The clock on the wall of the gym is made to measure for this. Its face is mapped out in two simple sections. From noon to nine o'clock is one segment. That's three minutes. From nine to noon is the minute's rest. The fighter is a slave to the clock. He will skip for three minutes, rest for one, skip again for three. He will punch the speedball for three minutes, rest for one, punch again for three. Exercise on the floor for three, rest for one, exercise again. Shadow-box in the ring for three minutes, rest for one, shadow-box again. Spar with a partner for three, rest for one, spar again. The routine is relentless. Calculated and cruel. It is total discipline. Nothing less will do.

Boxing demands frightening mental and physical discipline. Ability to withstand pain, desire to administer it. Courage to fight on when reason tells you to stop. Flexibility of mind to think ahead and plan when legs, arms and brain are skirting disaster. Resilience to accept defeat and believe in victory. All this must come from obedience to the recurring theme: three minutes, one minute, three minutes, master-minded by the clock on the wall of the gym. The unremitting discipline of training is what, in the end, kills a fighter's desire to fight.

A fighter gets out of his bed at 5am or earlier, summer and winter, to do his roadwork, pounding the local streets or the paths of a park, before the cars are out and about, belching their fumes at him. Five miles, maybe, of lonely running. If you're lucky, there is the trainer on his bike or following in a car, to keep you company. After running, home to breakfast, then off to work, unless you happen to be a star who can live off his ring earnings. If your employer is understanding or you have a part-time job, home again at one to collect the gear, then off to the gym. Now comes the two-hour training stint. Fighters vary in their routines and the order they complete them. But sparring is the core of the work, together with assorted exercises.

Randolph Turpin toughened his stomach muscles by lying on the floor, bracing himself, then getting his trainer to hurl a heavy medicine ball with all his strength straight into his midriff. Turpin could take body punches all night long. Sonny Liston eased the monotony of skipping by doing it in time with a rock tune called *Night Train*. Some achieve a magical fluency on the pear-shaped speed-ball, rat-a-tatting on it with perfect metronome timing. Others, less co-ordinated, stutter and stop . . . stutter and stop. Archie Moore, in the years he was chasing Rocky Marciano for a shot at the heavy-weight crown, stuck a likeness of Marciano on the heavy bag and slammed at it with all his might to offload frustration. When the time came, he hit Marciano for real, just as hard, but it made no difference. Archie lost.

The perpetual cry in the gym is: 'Last ten!' This is the urgent squawk of the trainer as the three-minute round nears its end. It means ten seconds to go, work harder, put in the big effort, NOW! before the bell ends the round. It's the call to drag out that little bit of extra effort. Every trainer I know inevitably calls it, not with ten seconds to go, but nearer thirty.

When gym-work is done, a shower, then back home to dinner, the main meal of the day. Most fighters doggedly stick to steaks, roasts, green vegetables, grilled fish and pints of milk. Alongside bacon-and-eggs and orange juice for breakfast, they are the mainstay of the boxer's diet. The thinking is traditional and old-fashioned. But perhaps in the end it is best to stick with what you believe does you the most good. Heavyweights have few problems with food and drink. Boxers in other

Charlie Magri touching his toes in Terry Lawless's Canning Town headquarters.

The gym is boxing's workshop, or, more exactly, sweatshop. But here there is companionship. You work with your mates around you. If you belong to the London stable of Terry Lawless, you train in Lawless's own gym, above the Royal Oak pub in dockland. Jim Watt, Maurice Hope, Charlie Magri, Kirkland Laing, Sylvester Mittee—all these famous boxers are managed by Lawless. It's just possible you could find them all training here at the same time.

Skipping is one of the most popular exercises. It helps co-ordination and encourages nimble footwork that will be used to avoid punches on the night. Some boxers have developed skipping almost to an art-form. The late Eric Boon, former British lightweight champion, was so adept it became entertainment. There is no set pattern to a boxer's training routine. Boxers may work out their own sequence of events or stick to the pattern they were first taught as amateurs. The important thing is to have a well-balanced routine, working on the points that need most attention. The most vital part of training is: make sure you do it.

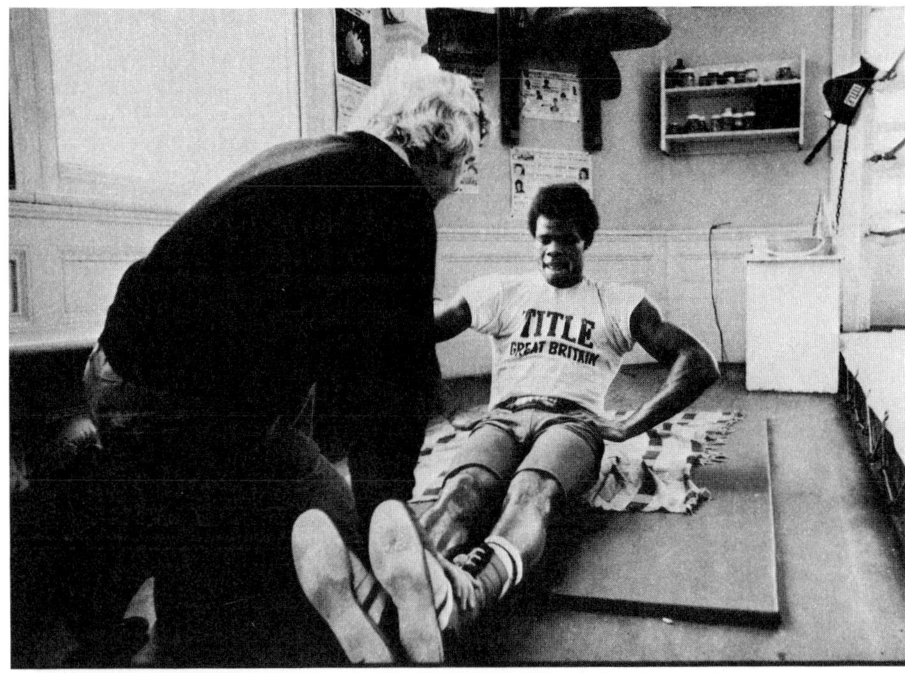

Laing doing sit-ups, with trainer Frank Black holding the legs in place.

Magri doing squat jumps under the gaze of the watch-holder. Everything in the gym is patterned to three minutes' work and one minute's rest, the same as a fight. Sometimes the minute's rest is cut to 30 seconds in the gym, on the theory that, when it comes, fight-night will seem a pushover.

divisions always have to care about their weight. They are required to make a certain poundage at 1 pm on the day of the fight. There is no escape. It has to be done. Titles are forfeited, careers ruined by failure to make the proper weight. It can be an insoluble problem.

Shadow-boxing before the mirror . . . working out the combinations of punches that will be thrown for real on the night. The mirror helps to check on poise and balance and get the 'feel' right. Shadow-boxing is also done in the ring where you can learn to use the ropes when backing up.

For example, the straightforward process of growing forces a man out of one division, where he is champion, into another where he must start climbing all over again. Reluctance to do this causes fighters tortures of deprivation. The first thing sacrificed is liquid intake. I have known champions,

Sparring—or mock-boxing—is the basic element of training. This is where moves are tested, techniques improved, and stamina built. A fighter in training may spar three, six, nine, or very exceptionally even 15 rounds a day. A hundred rounds of sparring in preparation for a title fight is not uncommon. Sometimes sparring sessions will flare into real battles, but generally a champion treats his sparring-partners with care and respect, taking no liberties. Lawless's boxers usually spar with each other, but if a sparring-partner with a special style is required, he may be hired and paid for his services by the round.

desperate not to relinquish money-making titles, deny themselves a drink of water for days on end. They come to the scales on the day of the fight and make the weight. But their strength has gone. Weak as a kitten, they are KOd in the opening round. Attempting to make an unnatural weight is one of the gravest threats to a fighter's well-being. It still goes on.

Fighters in training are generally in bed by 10pm, but not necessarily a lonely bed. The

The gloves are off and Laing unwinds the protective bandages. His training day is almost done.

ancient shibboleth against sexual activity has been swept aside: if indeed it was ever properly obeyed. What about Harry Greb, the American, who entertained chorus-girls in his dressing-room in the 1920s, right up to the moment he walked out for a fight? Greb seemed to thrive on it. He was middleweight champion of the world and the only man ever to beat Gene Tunney. Today sex is regarded by most trainers as a normal part of life and fighters are trusted to behave sensibly about it. They are not encouraged to do a Harry Greb.

The modern approach perhaps would not have suited the late Matt Wells. Matt was born in 1886, was ABA champion four years running in the early years of this century, became British professional lightweight champion and fought for years in Australia and America. He was, in fact, one of our greatest boxers. I knew Matt in his declining years when he was coaching youngsters at a London school. I shall never forget his scorn one day when he caught a boy dusting himself with talcum powder after a shower. 'Talcum powder!' snorted Matt. 'Gawd blimey, if that gets in 'is system, 'eaven 'elp 'im!' No, I don't think Matt would have approved of sex in training.

I have never had the nerve to ask a fighter whether the clock on the wall of the gym still haunts him when he climbs into bed. Does his wife ever whisper: 'Last ten'?

Overpage
Sylvester Mittee with the headguard that's used for sparring. It protects the face from injury, particularly around the eyes, the most vulnerable area. A big pay-day can be lost through injury in training. The gum-shield, which stops the teeth being forced through the lips, is just going in.

CHAPTER SIX
THE ICEBERG

All over Britain, professional boxers train in small gyms. Tommy Miller has a gym in Bradford and from here he dispatches his fighters anywhere they are needed, usually at small promotions.

Right
Fighters approach the anonymous facade of Tommy Miller's gym.
Centre
Training in Miller's gym is earnest, but lacks the glamour that surrounds the famous Lawless camp.
Far Right
The unsung fighter, the backbone of the sport. John Lindo, a lightweight in his early 20s, turned pro with Miller in 1979 and in his first year fought in Liverpool, Hartlepool, Birmingham, Sheffield, Bolton, Nantwich, Glasgow, and Bradford, where he comes from. His record is patchy. In one fight he was knocked out in 75 seconds, and in his next he stopped his opponent in less than two minutes.

The crowd is expectant. The Big Fight is almost on. In the corners, six-ounce gloves are being pulled on and laced. In the crowd, last-second bets are struck. The referee stands alone below the ring, waiting to be called. But first, the MC must go through The Ritual. The Ritual is the formal introduction of 'some of the outstanding personalities with us here tonight'. It's a way of stoking the atmosphere, encouraging the crowd to stretch their vocal chords, bang their hands in applause. It's the warm-up and it works. One after the other, old champions come up, jack-knife themselves through the ropes, smile and wave to the crowd, step respectfully to both corners to tap the gloves and mutter: 'All the best, mate.'

For a few happy moments the old champions are back where they belong, in the ring, warmed again by the lights and the emotion spreading to them from the crowd. The Ritual is popular. It's the right hors d'oeuvre before the main

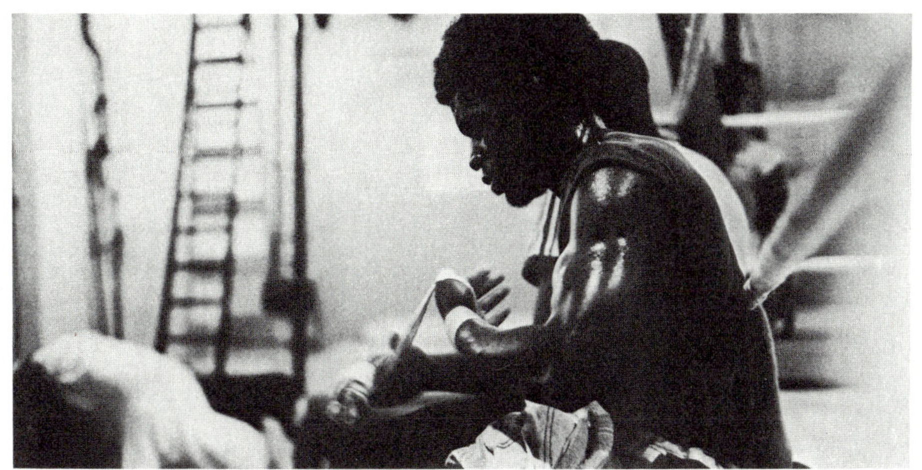

Like most small-time pro boxers, Lindo combines his sport with a day-to-day job. It's hard. John assembles TV visual-display screens. He gets to the gym at seven in the evening, having done a day's work, and trains for about an hour and a half. It's after 9pm before he returns home. In 1980 he fought nine times, with three wins, two draws, four defeats.

course. In England, Henry Cooper, Terry Downes and Larry Gains sometimes draw bigger cheers than the participants themselves. In Scotland, Peter Keenan, Walter McGowan, Ken Buchanan may do the same. In Wales, it's Howard Winstone, Eddie Thomas or Jack Petersen. And in Ireland, Rinty Monaghan, Freddie Gilroy, Johnny Caldwell. . . .

If the deeds were great enough, the personality appealing enough, an old champion can build a lucrative post-fight career. One or two will become superstars, opening fetes, playing golf pro-ams, turning up on *Parkinson*, taking the guest-of-honour seat at dinners. Just one or two. Boxing is an iceberg, the public see only the tip of it. For every winner, there is a loser, for every champion, dozens of also-rans whose names will never catch on. Boxing is full of anonymous triers. How else could the game run? How can any sport flourish without its quota of also-rans? But because boxing is

The man who's seen it all: Miller's face tells you he's done a bit himself. Those cups behind him were won in his days as a fighter. He claims to have had 'about 1,000 fights', in Blackpool booths and with travelling fairs.

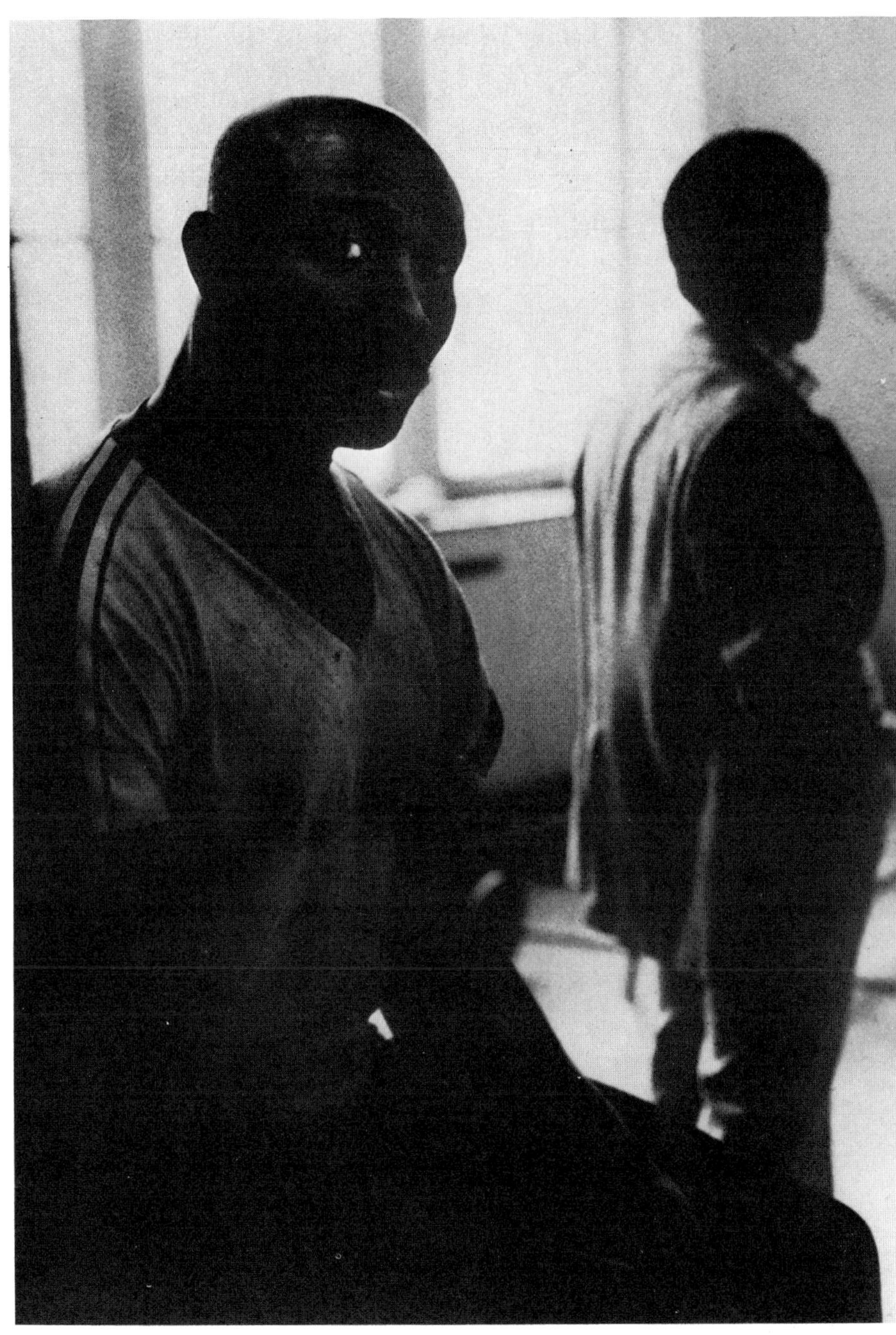

The trainer, whose job it is to make fighters like John Lindo into worthy contestants.

Lindo's trainer is wearing punch-pads. He lets Lindo aim punches at his hands and picks them off. In this way he can teach his boxer new moves without actually sparring with him.

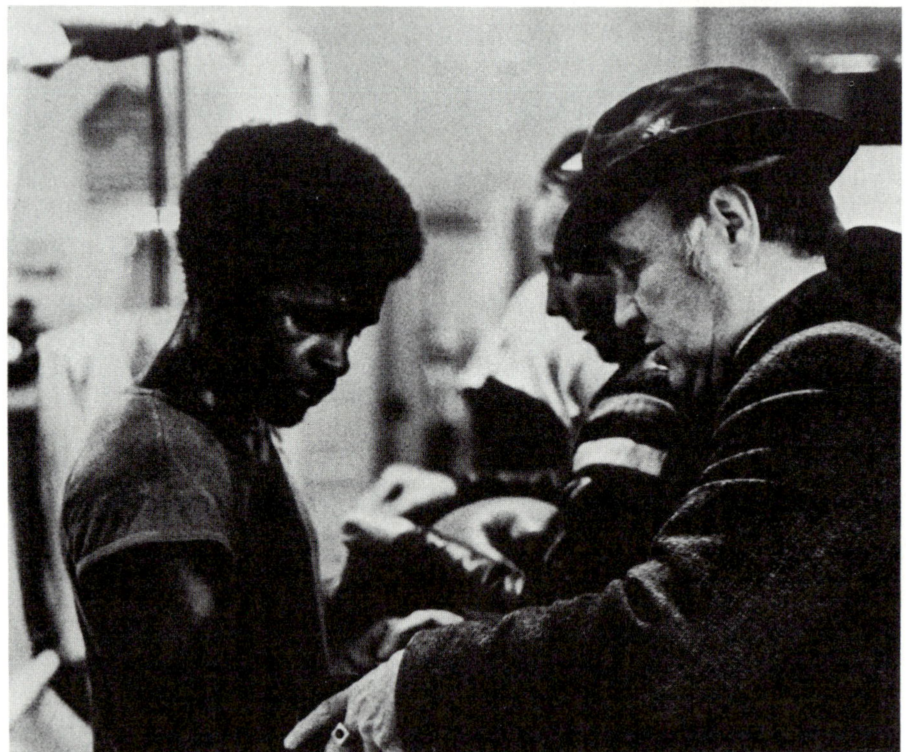

Miller helps Lindo get the gloves off. Tommy Miller, jaunty hat jammed on head, even in the gym, is very much an 'old-school' manager, a one-man business, more concerned with getting fights for his boxers than with actually coaching them.

Miller at home, in his usual pose: on the phone. It rings day and night. Sometimes Mickey Duff will call from London and request a boxer for that night. Miller can comply. That's his business. His fighters are ready to go anywhere, at a moment's notice—provided they have understanding employers.

so hard, demanding and full of hurt, the plight of the faceless ones seems that much more desperate.

The Hardest Game would not survive a week unless, in cities and towns throughout the country, the gyms were full of men, black and white, in their twenties, sometimes in their thirties, who still believe in miracles. They have to believe they've got the talent to go to the top, that one day they will be that Big Guy in the well-cut suit and hand-stitched shoes, signing the autographs. But what about that dreadful moment when truth dawns, as inevitably it must?

It surely comes at night, perhaps in an improvised dressing-room in the basement of a posh London hotel, where the smell of the nearby kitchen permeates and suffocates. The anonymous trier has just lost another run-of-the-mill fight out there in the great dining-room, where the ring is set among drink-laden tables, where dinner-suited spectators watched him struggle, never bothering with his name – 'I'll take 5–4 and have the one in red.' He lost. Decisively. But he can't understand it: 'The other fellow hardly laid a glove on me. That ref never done me any favours, I tell you.' His body aches for rest and he has a face full of bruises.

He was up at six o'clock that morning, did half a day's work, met his manager in the afternoon, climbed into the car and came from Liverpool to London. Stopped for a bite of something lousy on the motorway. Didn't get to the hotel until half-past seven. Went in the ring at half-past ten. Now it's past eleven. He's a loser in London and home is in Liverpool. The pursemoney – £100 – won't stretch to a room for the night. Besides, he's due back at the factory in the morning. So, get changed, stuff the gear in the holdall, throw it in the boot, curl up on the back seat of the manager's old banger and try to grab some sleep on the long grind up the motorway.

He is back in the house as dawn breaks. Wake up the wife with the embarrassing admission once again: 'Yeah, I lost, but that ref doesn't know what day it is.' Breakfast, clock-on for a working day and go through the same excuses.

Perhaps somewhere on that grim night journey north a cold voice inside him whispered: 'This is how it's always going to be. Don't kid yourself. You're never going to be a champion. There's never going to be stardom, money, headlines. You're a loser.'

Later that week, the manager's on the phone to him: 'I've got this offer for another fight down south in ten days' time. Only a hundred quid, but I think you can take this guy. They tell me he's just a raw beginner. You can handle him. Fancy it?'

Yes. He fancies it. This one will be different. He has to believe in miracles.

Phil Duckworth, of Leeds, former amateur champion of the North-Eastern Counties, is one of Miller's men. He started his pro career in 1980 with a string of wins.

Above:
Phil works as a welder.
Above right
Fortunately, his employer is boxing-mad.

Miller has got Duckworth a fight in Newcastle, on a dinner-and-boxing bill at the Gosforth Park Hotel. Duckworth is top of the bill and the hotel have given him one of their bedrooms as a dressing-room, so he warms up in front of the TV set.

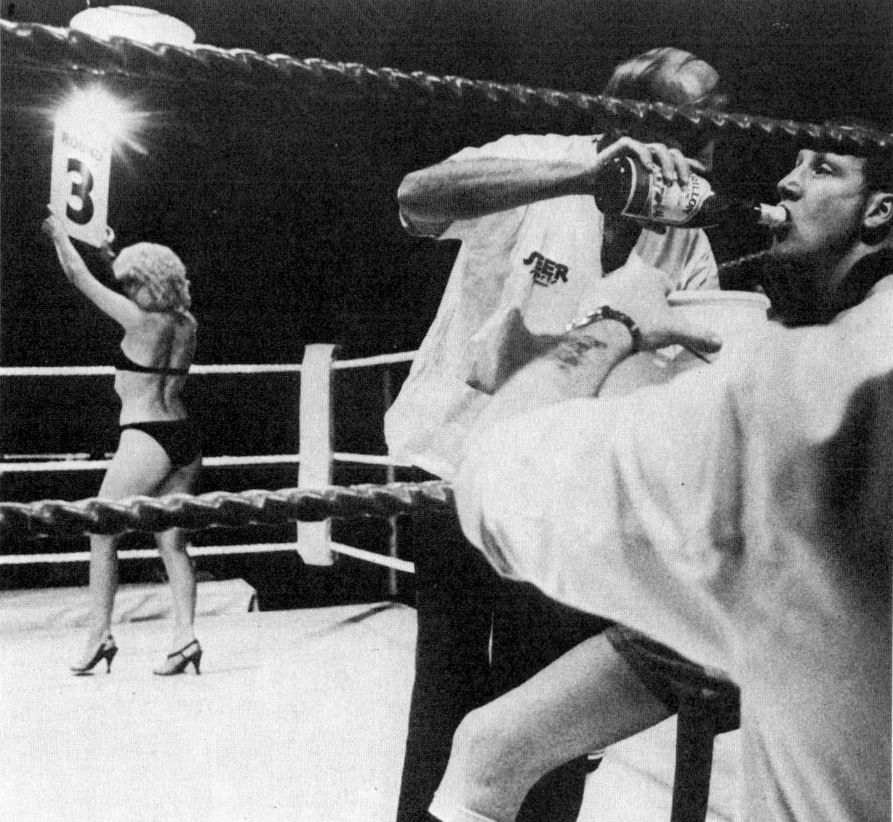

Above left
Duckworth sits and waits to be called for his fight. The hotel lounge has been set aside as a waiting area.

Above
In the hotel dining-room, the ring is occupied by the statutory comedian. In the old days boxing fans were happy to go to the local fight arena and just watch boxing. Now it's on with the dinner-jacket and out to the hotel, with food, wine and blue jokes as hors d'oeuvres before the punches fly.

When the boxing does start, the round numbers must be hoisted by the obligatory sex-symbol. Sometimes you get the impression that boxing is not really the point of the evening.

Inset
The cornerman wonders which way it's going and the round-number girl tries to look interested.

Duckworth's opponent is Billy Bryce of Sunderland, having only his third pro fight. It's hard and close all the way.
Inset
Fred Potter the referee lifts Duckworth's hand. Potter has scored it 79—78½, just one round's margin in Phil's favour.

Inset
Am I still pretty? Like every fighter, Duckworth seeks out a mirror and inspects for damage. On this night, there was nothing to worry about.

The next day Miller went to the factory where Duckworth works, to pay him his purse-money. Miller took him into the bathroom to hand the money over.

CHAPTER SEVEN
THE BIG CHANCE

Colin Jones pounds away up a hill near Merthyr. He's four days away from the big fight with Kirkland Laing at Wembley for the British welterweight championship.

Miracles sometimes happen. Colin Jones once dug graves for a living in his native Wales. He could box a bit and punch much better. He belonged to the Penyrheol club in Gorseinon, near Swansea. Colin, fair of hair, made steady progress through the amateur ranks, winning Welsh schoolboy and junior titles. He even won a national schools title three years running. His elder brother Ken was a useful boxer, too. But the Jones boys lived too far from London to excite the 'smart' set, the gents who sniff out talent and draw it into the net.

In 1976 Colin Jones, just turned 17 and in only his second contest as a senior amateur, won the Welsh welterweight championship. Then he went to Manchester and won the ABA semi-final. Two weeks later he travelled up from Wales to Wembley for the final, his fourth senior bout, against the well-known Navy man, Paul Kelly, captain of England's international team. You could almost hear the buzz

Laing's challenger has just celebrated his 21st birthday. His manager, Eddie Thomas, in the car, has never before been able to get Jones on a big London show. Thomas doesn't hit it off with the London promoters. Yet Jones, twice an ABA champion, has won all 13 professional fights and with his undoubted big punch has stopped all but three of his opponents inside the distance. The fact remains, Jones is hardly known outside Wales.

going round Wembley: 'Who's Jones?' Unknown Welsh boxers cut no ice in London. But he won. ABA champion after four senior contests? That is rare. In his next contest he was back at Wembley, representing Great Britain against the United States. Ralph Fratto, champion of the US Army from Fort Bragg, North Carolina, was going nicely in the third and final round when he walked on to Jones's right. Fratto dropped to the floor. A few moments later the referee stepped in and stopped it. Senior bout No. 5. Number six took place in Montreal in the Olympic Games.

Colin, still only 17, the youngest member of Britain's Olympic team, outscored an Irishman and then, in senior bout No. 7, came up against Victor Zilberman, 28, five times champion of Rumania, boxing in his third Olympics. Jones went three rounds with him and lost on points. He returned to Wales for a further period of obscurity.

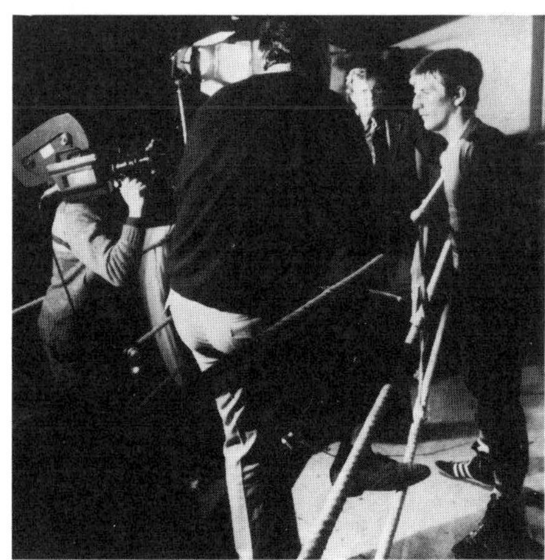

Colin may not be a name in London, but in Wales he's a celebrity and local-TV are there to watch him train in the old school gym in Merthyr, where Eddie Thomas has his HQ.

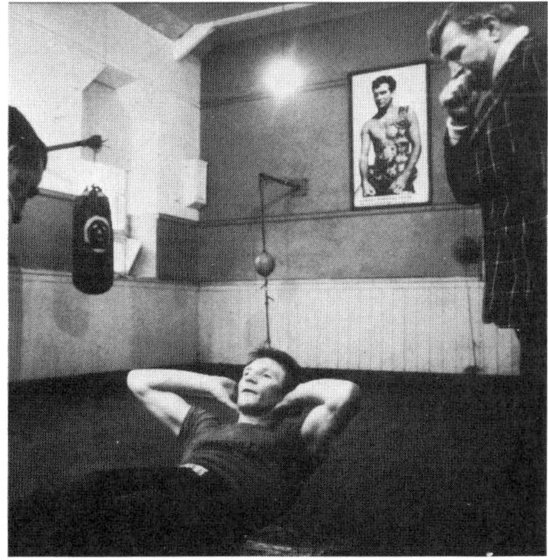

Thomas and trainer supervise the sit-ups. On the wall, a picture of Howard Winstone, the most successful boxer Thomas ever managed. Winstone, a superb boxer despite having the tops of fingers missing on one hand, won the world featherweight championship in 1968. Thomas believes he can take Jones to the world welterweight title.

Previous pages
Jones spars with the man he's hired especially for this fight: Achille 'Speedy' Mitchell, an experienced pro from the Midlands. Mitchell has been brought in because he knows Laing's style. Eighteen months earlier, Laing had to overcome Mitchell before he could box for the British title. Now Mitchell is giving Jones an idea of the way Laing will work.

The following year, still a novice in terms of senior boxing, he went through most of it again: won the Welsh title, the ABA semi-final and the big one at Wembley. The wide boys in London still took no notice. Whether they wrote him off as a fluke winner, I don't know. Later that year, 1977, he signed professional with the Merthyr manager, Eddie Thomas. Eddie, a master boxer in his day, was not exactly in love with the smart boys in London. For years he had operated outside their fashionable circle. Eddie was a great mate of Jack Solomons, who had promoted all his big championship fights years before. But Solomons was no longer the big wheel in London and although Thomas's fighters frequently appeared at Jack's swish World Sporting Club at Grosvenor House in Park Lane, they seldom if ever turned up at Wembley or the Albert Hall.

Right
In London's East End, just another workday in the Terry Lawless gym. While Kirkland Laing (white vest) spars with Sylvester Mittee, in preparation for his fight with Jones, Charlie Magri, flyweight champion of Britain and Europe, carries on skipping.

Top right
Laing is 24, lives in Nottingham, but comes to London to train for big fights. A former ABA champion, he has enviable boxing skill, but gets criticized for his too-relaxed attitude. This will be his first defence of the British title. In five years he has never lost a professional fight.

Above left
Sunday morning, and Laing is a lonely figure in the changing-room of the vast Victoria Park, Hackney, where he runs—on his own.

Above
The day of the fight, just before 1 o'clock. Jones and Thomas arrive for the weigh-in at the Horseshoe pub in Tottenham Court Road.

So for two years Colin Jones, thick-set and aggressive, thumped his way through the opposition in Caerphilly, Aberavon and Plymouth. When he was training for fights he would pop down each day to the local railway station to check his weight on the freight scales. He won 13 fights straight off (in 10 of them his opponent failed to last the distance) until the Boxing Board nominated him as challenger for his manager's old title, the British welterweight championship, held by Kirkland Laing, of Nottingham. Laing, like Jones, had won the ABA championship and then been snapped up by Terry Lawless and brought to London. He was not one of Lawless's best-known boxers or one of his best-disciplined. But he was British champion.

On 1 April 1980, Colin Jones appeared on a major London commercial show for the first time since he went pro in 1976. His challenge to Laing

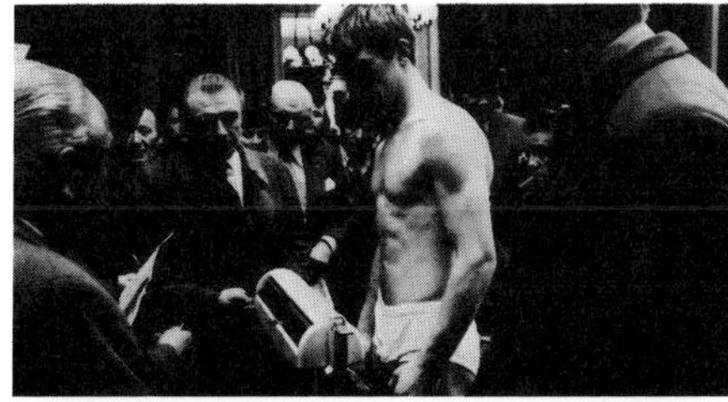

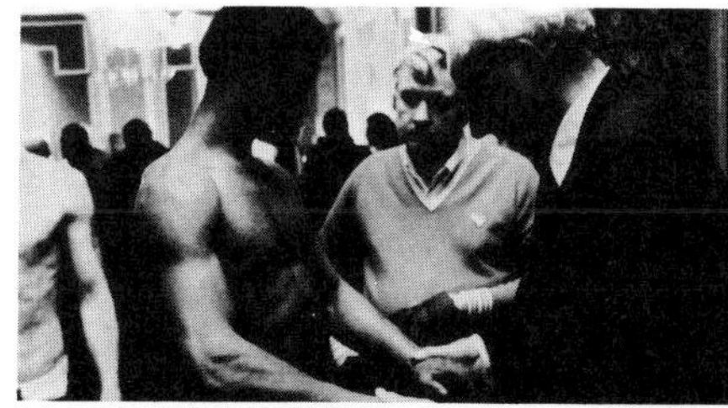

Left
Laing is checked by a Board of Control doctor.
Far left
Jones weighs 10st 5¼lb, twelve ounces lighter than the champion. On the far side, Terry Lawless, Laing's manager, watches. In the foreground, right, is co-promoter Mike Barrett.

Above left
Thomas and Jones keep to themselves after the weigh-in. Jones is very much the new boy from out-of-town. But Boxing News, *the London-based trade paper, has given him a huge boost. Its preview of the fight is headlined: 'The Jones Boy can grab Laing's crown', and their writer says: 'It is a very difficult fight to predict . . . but, tentatively, it seems most likely that Jones will walk through Laing's better shots and prove too strong for him, gaining victory around the 10th.'*
Above right
Laing, off to his final meal before the fight, has read the preview, but seems unconcerned.

Right
At the Conference Centre, Wembley, the fight is under way. From the corner, Eddie Thomas & Co see their man fall way behind. For round after round, Laing boxes like a champion. After eight rounds, he's a mile ahead. The crowd is convinced Laing will keep his title. Only in Jones's corner does a little bit of hope remain.

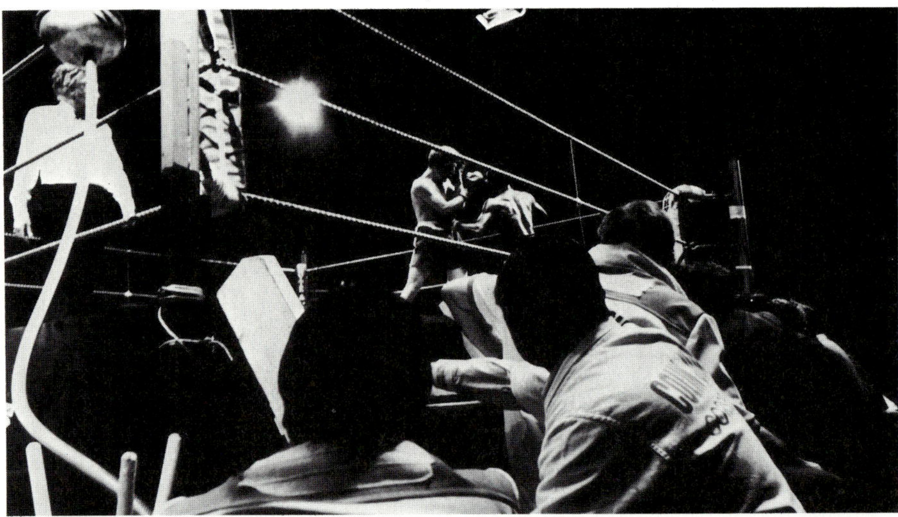

Centre (both)
The first minute of the ninth round . . . Jones fires his big right hand. Laing, off-guard, is caught smack on the chin. His gumshield flies from his mouth and lands in the third row. His knees buckle. But he doesn't go down.

Right
Jones knows his big change has come and attacks non-stop.

Left
Jones is throwing punches from all angles. Laing's resistance is crumbling. Roland Dakin, the referee, begins to worry about him.

Centre left
Dakin has seen enough. Laing is still upright, but totally confused. Jones, winner of 14 fights in a row, appearing on his first major London show, is Britain's new welterweight champion.
Centre right
Jones realizes what a triumph it is, while Laing fumbles his way miserably to his corner. Boxing News *had got it just about right in their preview. Their man later writes: 'It was one of the most dramatic turn-abouts I've seen.'*

Above
Thomas scratches his head. Perhaps he doesn't believe it himself. Suddenly his war with London's top promoters is over. They want his boy now. The Lonsdale Belt is already round Jones's waist. He won't keep it unless he wins three British title fights at the same weight.

Above
One of the first to congratulate Jones is 'Speedy' Mitchell, the man who helped him fathom Laing's style. Mitchell says, over and over again: 'I told you so. I told you so . . .' With just one punch, Jones has won national fame, the sort of story that gives boxing its universal appeal.

took place at Wembley's slick, new, air-conditioned Conference Centre, alongside the Arena where he had twice won the ABA title and dropped the man from the United States Army. Even now, in 1980, you could still sense the buzz: 'Who's Jones?' Tucked away in the programme notes was a quote from Eddie Thomas: 'Colin is something special. If a champion comes out of Wales he's usually above average and I feel that's going to stay true with Colin.' Who reads programme notes?

Laing is an artistic boxer with a lot of flair. Looking at my scorecard now I see that in the first eight rounds I marked two even. The rest I gave to Laing. It really was no race. Jones, square-built, short-armed, bursting with aggression, was getting an old-fashioned boxing lesson. It seemed as if the gravedigger had had his one glimpse of the big time. Tomorrow morning, bumped and bruised, he'd be back in the valleys, nursing his pride. He might even wind up digging graves again.

In the ninth, Jones threw his right hand, the one that had dumped Fratto. Laing caught it on the chin and wobbled. Jones attacked savagely. Seconds later, the referee was waving his arms over the stricken Laing and Britain had a new welterweight champion.

Eddie Thomas was a very happy man. The smart boys? They must have wondered why they hadn't noticed Jones before.

CHAPTER EIGHT
DAY OF THE BIG FIGHT

It's Friday, the morning of the big fight in Glasgow's massive Kelvin Hall. Local hero Jim Watt is defending his WBC lightweight championship tonight against Northern Ireland's Charlie Nash. The ring has just been installed. Contractors discuss with the fight's Press officer how ringside benches are to be laid out.

In *South Pacific* they sang 'There is Nothing like a Dame'. Someone should compose a song for boxing: 'There is Nothing like a Fight' —a big fight, that is, a *really* big fight. The day of the big fight has a feel, smell and taste all its own. It has everything to do with the long wait. The fight won't be on until 9 or 10 at night, possibly even later if it's going over the TV satellite to America. There is a whole day to think about it and savour the atmosphere.

A city with a big fight is taken over for the day by the fight crowd, together with many more who won't be there for the fight, but insist on being part of the build-up. At the core of the day's pleasureable laziness is the weigh-in. For a really big fight a cinema is hired with its hundreds of seats for lookers-on. When Cassius Clay came to fight Henry Cooper in 1963 the weigh-in was staged at the London Palladium. Argyll Street was jammed with sightseers. Clay, still some months away from winning the world title, appeared on stage where the scales were placed, clad in a dressing-gown with the words 'Cassius Clay the Greatest' flaring from the back. Behind the scenes, among the prop-baskets, Clay discovered a cardboard crown of gold, left from a pantomime, and requisitioned it. He wore it that night at Wembley Stadium as he strutted to and from the ring. It was the sort of arrogant jest that riled people in those days. Looking back, it wasn't so much a boast as an affirmation of his rightful place in the heavyweight kingdom. Less than a year later, he *was* king of the ring and remained so for a good part of our lives.

The weigh-in is pure ceremonial. It takes place at 1pm and the faithful flock to it. The upright, white balance scales stand imposingly at the centre, like an altar. They have been checked for evenness with a spirit-level, for accuracy with standard weights. The public drift in to their seats. There is no charge, unless a token fee is taken for charity. The initiated gather on the stage, jostling for position near the altar. So do photographers and reporters. Scant interest is taken in the weights of the supporting boxers as they shuffle to and fro, whipping their underpants off and on. Ladies, you will gather, are not encouraged to attend, although some do. Television may be there, if the fight is big enough (Marvin Hagler, the American world middleweight champion, was the first fighter to appear naked on BBC screens when he weighed in for his fight with Alan Minter).

As the moment nears for the entrance of the main contestants, the crowd at the altar swells to twice its size and the MC makes the time-honoured plea: 'Will all those people not involved with the fight kindly move off the stage?' Not a soul moves. The fighters appear, their faces lit with the flash of cameras. They may come to the scales together or separately. There is no laid-down order of precedence, but usually the champion prefers to weigh second. After all, he is supposed to be the star of the show and should provide the climax. As each man steps out of his shoes and on to the scales, a Board of Control inspector slides the measure along the bar. The Board secretary watches over him. The two managers crane forward, peering hard at the measuring, giving the firm impression that their men are liable to be the victims of some unspeakable skullduggery. As each man steps back off the scales to have his robe wrapped around him, his weight is called. Click, whirr, flash. Pencils scribble in notebooks. Agency men and those who work for evening papers dash for phones. Soon the stop-press columns throughout the land will carry the vital news. The public leave their seats and wander out into daylight and the real world, explaining learnedly to each other the significance of what they've just seen and heard.

For the boxer, the day of the fight – the really big fight – drags itself out, an unpleasant nauseous mixture of utter boredom and gnawing anxiety. He sleeps late, does a few loosening-up exercises, ambling his way through the morning until it's time to leave the hotel and make for the weigh-in. He tries not to look too much at his opponent, but he will sneak a peep to check if the other man is feeling worse than he is. He will be grabbed by Press, radio and TV for a quick quote.

The inevitable triviality of what he has to say doesn't matter. Then he is hustled out past the waiting crowds as fast as possible and away to the main meal of the day.

After that? He kills time as best he can, the way it suits him. Sleep. Cards. TV. Reading. Or perhaps a restless, wordless wakefulness, worrying if he's done enough training, or the right sort of training, and running through his mind his own action pre-play of the fight. These are awful hours for some, child's play to others. Around him his cornermen pack his bag and sort the towels. They assemble the emergency kit of swabsticks, gauze, scissors, adrenalin, vaseline and icebag. They tape the water-bottle so it won't slip from hurried, nervous fingers. The moment to leave for the fight comes as a blessed relief from the brooding tension. In the stadium dressing-room he flops on the couch and reads telegrams from friends and relations. He can hear the crowd applauding early fights. He may have a stablemate on the bill, sharing his room. When the stablemate returns from the ring there's an anxious: 'How did it go?' A win is a good omen. Defeat hangs heavy in the air and creates more tension.

The door is locked. It is opened grudgingly only to those closest to him or those on official business. The trainer cuts his strips of sticky tape and arranges them in orderly rows on the

Top left
The carpenters are happy. They've laid the ring floor.
Top right
Rinty Monaghan, former flyweight champion of the world, has come over from Belfast to see how Nash makes out. Rinty, who used to sing to the crowd after his fights, scores a hit with the cleaning ladies.
Upper centre
A BBC-TV engineer takes a seat in the corner to study the position of his lighting. If he doesn't get it right, the viewers won't get good pictures. At the back of the hall, the sponsors of the fight have already fixed one of their signs in place. He won't be lighting that.
Centre right
Immaculate layout for a big fight. This is the ring the public never sees. Bare wooden planks await their covering of safety mat and canvas.
Lower centre
Press seats, phones in place. It looks neat and simple, but somewhere under that ring a Post Office engineer is groping around in the dark, sorting out cables and connections.

Timekeeper's position, with bell and microphone. He brings his own stopwatches.

Ex-fighters inevitably gather, only too eager to talk over old times.

__Top left__
The top-brass arrives and claims its place in the ring. Wearing glasses, co-promoter Mike Barrett is up from London with his partner, Mickey Duff, who leans on the ropes with Jarvis Astaire, Mr Viewsport, the closed-circuit TV entrepreneur who masterminds satellite transmission of big fights to and from the United States.
__Top right__
Joe Aitchison, Glasgow fight trainer, a wee wizard of the game with trenchant views on the way the sport is run.
__Upper centre__
It's 1pm, weigh-in time. The throng inside the ropes is almost as crowded as the one outside. The ring groans under the weight of nearly fifty people. Nash, the challenger, is on the scales. Watt, the champion, alongside him, seems remarkably relaxed. To the left of Watt, with promoter Barrett, is Terry Lawless, Watt's London manager. Their partnership didn't begin until Watt was 27 and seemingly near the end of his career. It has proved a brilliant success.
__Lower centre__
Some seven hours later, Watt arrives for the fight. The Kelvin Hall dressing-room is bare and, for the moment, blissfully quiet. Trainer Frank Black hopes to keep it that way.
__Centre left__
The first customers arrive. Police are on duty at all points. Because of the Protestant v. Catholic nature of the fight, mob violence is feared.

Nash's room is suddenly alive with friends. A Scottish doctor makes a last-minute check.

Lawless passes over a giant good-luck message to Watt from dozens of Glasgow schoolkids.

BBC-TV, ready for action at ringside. Bruce Allen, of the Scottish outside broadcast team, smoothes the way for the commentator. Outside the hall, in his control van, Scotsman Bill Malcolm directs the TV transmission.

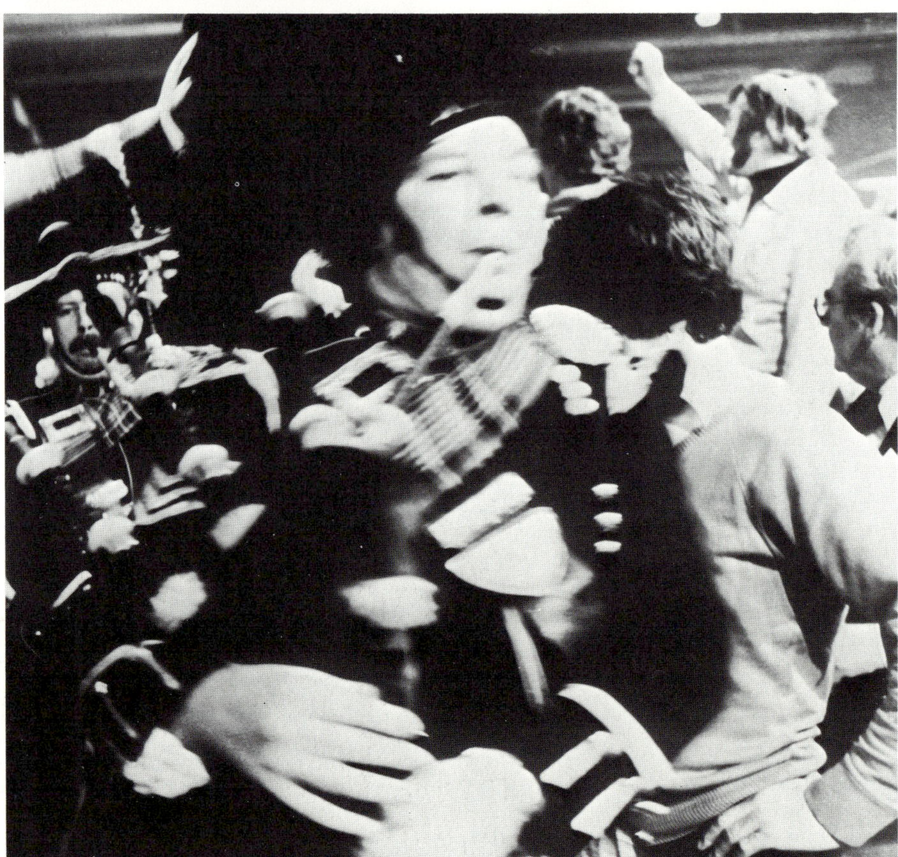

The moment everyone's waited for: the fighters move to the ring behind the skirl of Scottish pipes. The hall erupts with noise.

Watt, calm, carefully groomed. Behind him, veteran cornerman George Page, who works regularly with the Lawless camp.

Nash, hooded, and like those around him, understandably tense. The rest of his life will be influenced, one way or another, by what happens in the next few minutes.

Both boxers are in the ring, but for the moment photographers turn their backs to the ropes and concentrate on Margaret, Jim's wife.

mirror or the wall, ready to augment the bandages and keep them in place. An envoy from the other camp is permitted to come and supervise the bandaging of hands. When it's done, a Board inspector rubber-stamps the bandages to prevent later tampering. Outdoor clothes are shed; jock-strap, leather protective cup and satin trunks are

Right
Hush before the storm: only the voice of Nat Basso, the MC, is heard.

Far right
World title on the line: two southpaws face each other. It's been built as a 'grudge' fight. Watt says he has a score to settle because Nash has 'had a go at me, verbally'. But cold professionalism takes over once the bell sounds.

Nash starts well, and Watt goes down in the opening round. But he's up without a count.

donned, a towel wound round the neck and the dressing-gown either slipped on or draped across the shoulders. The gloves will be put on in the ring.

A knock on the door. 'OK, my son, here we go,' says the manager. The fighter walks out to meet the glare of the ring, the yell of the crowd. The long day is almost over.

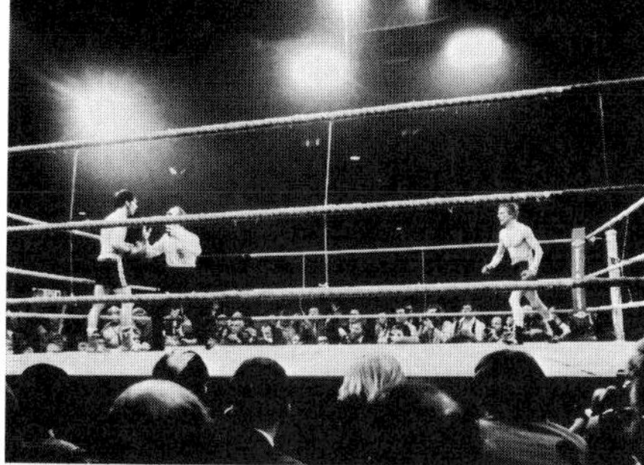

Far left
Watt says later: 'Once he hurt me, I knew I had to get him out of the way quickly.'
Left
By the fourth round, Nash is cut and in deep trouble. Watt has had him down.

The champion is looking for the finish.

Inset
Wherever Nash moves, Watt is chasing him. Nash has now been down twice.

The third time: referee Nathan knows what he must do.

Top left
It's over. Nathan plants himself protectively in front of Nash.

Top right
While Nash is led to his corner, Watt begins to celebrate. Lawless rushes to join him.

Centre left
Frank Black and Terry Lawless hoist their triumphant man, who crowns himself with the world championship trophy. Even George Page permits himself a grin. MC Basso tells everyone what they already know: Watt's won, and is still the WBC lightweight champion.

Centre right
The winner's view: an arena packed with happy fans. Nash's supporters have gone quietly.

A night to remember: Jim Watt enjoys it all with Margaret and son Andrew, who's donned Dad's winning gloves.

A night to forget: Charlie Nash must swallow his disappointment. To help him, plenty of spiritual solace, a rare sight in a fighter's dressing-room. The company is usually more down-to-earth.

CHAPTER NINE
SO NEAR AND YET...

The fight which will never be forgotten: in New York's Yankee Stadium, Welshman Tommy Farr is giving the immortal Joe Louis one of his hardest defences. The date: 1937. Nearly 50 years later, Farr is still a hero.

Only a choice few British boxers walk to the ring for the really Big Fight and come back winners. Our world champions down the years are a select group and they get their due praise. But the public have always shown affection for those who come close to the ultimate success without quite making it. How much more admired today would Henry Cooper be had he won the world heavyweight crown? His two losing fights with Ali, particularly the one in which he knocked Ali down (and that was not a title fight) have elevated Henry to the status of national hero. The public are not slow to realize that financial and social success have left Henry wearing precisely the same size in hats as when he started out plain Private Cooper, H., RAOC.

Tommy Farr, a miner from Tonypandy, is revered in the 1980s for the hour or so he spent at the sharp end of Joe Louis's mighty dangerous fists nearly half a century ago. In 1937, Farr set sail for New York as an alleged no-hoper, but by bringing years of experience and hardship to bear, he gave Louis one of his most difficult title defences. It still remains a mystery why this country, with its 250 years of boxing tradition – we are, after all, the founders of boxing – has been unable to produce a world heavyweight champion since the days of Bob Fitzsimmons at the end of the 19th century. Since Farr's superb effort, Don Cockell has taken on Rocky Marciano; Brian London has had a go at

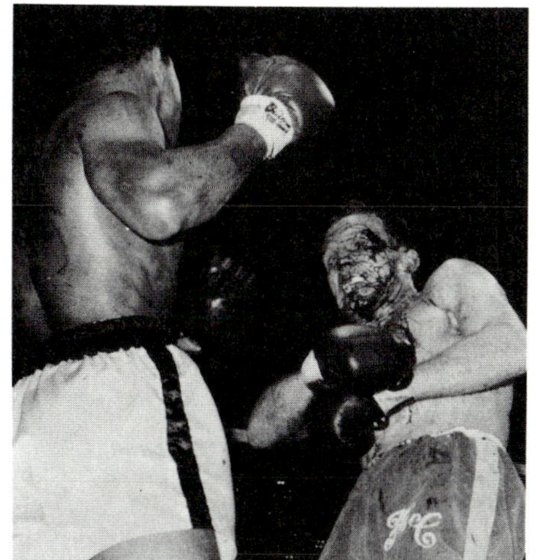

Far left
The end is near . . . Henry Cooper's cuts are impossibly bad. This fight at Highbury, 1966, is called off in round six. Muhammad Ali, then at his peak, remains champion.
Left
Joe Bugner, the most disappointing heavyweight of my time. Here in Las Vegas, 1973, he gives Muhammad Ali a good fight over 12 rounds. Later, in Malaysia, he takes Ali the distance again, this time for the world title. Joe lacked the one thing that might have made him world champion: the burning, passionate ambition of a great fighter.

The first world heavyweight championship I ever saw: no-one gave Britain's Don Cockell a chance with the fearsome Rocky Marciano (right), but in San Francisco, 1955, Don went nine rounds with him. Bravery, however, is never enough.

Floyd Patterson and Muhammad Ali; Henry Cooper, Joe Bugner and Richard Dunn have all had their crack at Ali. Yet we still wait for the big man with the right ability. I wonder. When he comes, will he be black, like almost every American heavyweight since Louis? I believe it is a strong possibility.

Some of our best white champions in the past, at all weights, have just fallen short of the ultimate success. The late Len Harvey, the most skilful and experienced British boxer of that prolific era just before World War II, was never able to win a world title. Harvey, a Cornishman like Bob Fitzsimmons, had his first paid fight in Plymouth when he was 13. He was paid five shillings.

He is the only man to have won British titles at middle, light-heavy and heavyweight. His boxing, like Farr's, was born from the years of the great depression when jobs were scarce. Today, in the '80s, we are seeing again a significant rise in the number of professional boxers as unemployment grows. But today this country is less naive than it was a half-century ago in its relationships with the rest of the boxing world. If Len Harvey were around today, he would without doubt win a world title, simply because he would be handled better, promoted better. We shall not see the like of Harvey again, but we are seeing less talented boxers going out into the world and winning the titles and massive acclaim that never came his way.

Ernie Roderick and Nel Tarleton were brothers-in-law from Liverpool, where their names conjure up a golden boxing age that has long since died in that great city. Both men attempted to win world titles before the last war, but failed. It is inconceivable, given their talent and modern boxing manoeuvres, that they would fail today. Welterweight Roderick went in the ring with the American super-champion Henry Armstrong at Harringay in 1939 and took him the full 15 rounds. Armstrong – known as 'Hammerin' Hank' – at one time held three world titles simultaneously, a unique achievement. Nel Tarleton is remembered for his two gallant attempts to take the world featherweight crown from the brilliant American Freddie Miller, possibly the best southpaw champion of all time. Both fights were held out of doors in Liverpool in the 1930s, both went 15 rounds and, by all accounts, the only thing that stopped Tarleton winning the second one was his lack of a damaging punch. That, plus the fact that Tarleton had only one sound lung. And yet he won two Lonsdale Belts. The 1920s and '30s were the age of giants in British boxing, but we have scant success to show for it. Since 1945, the story has been better.

Like Tarleton, Howard Winstone, the Welshman, was a fine featherweight suffering from a physical disability. He had the tops of three fingers

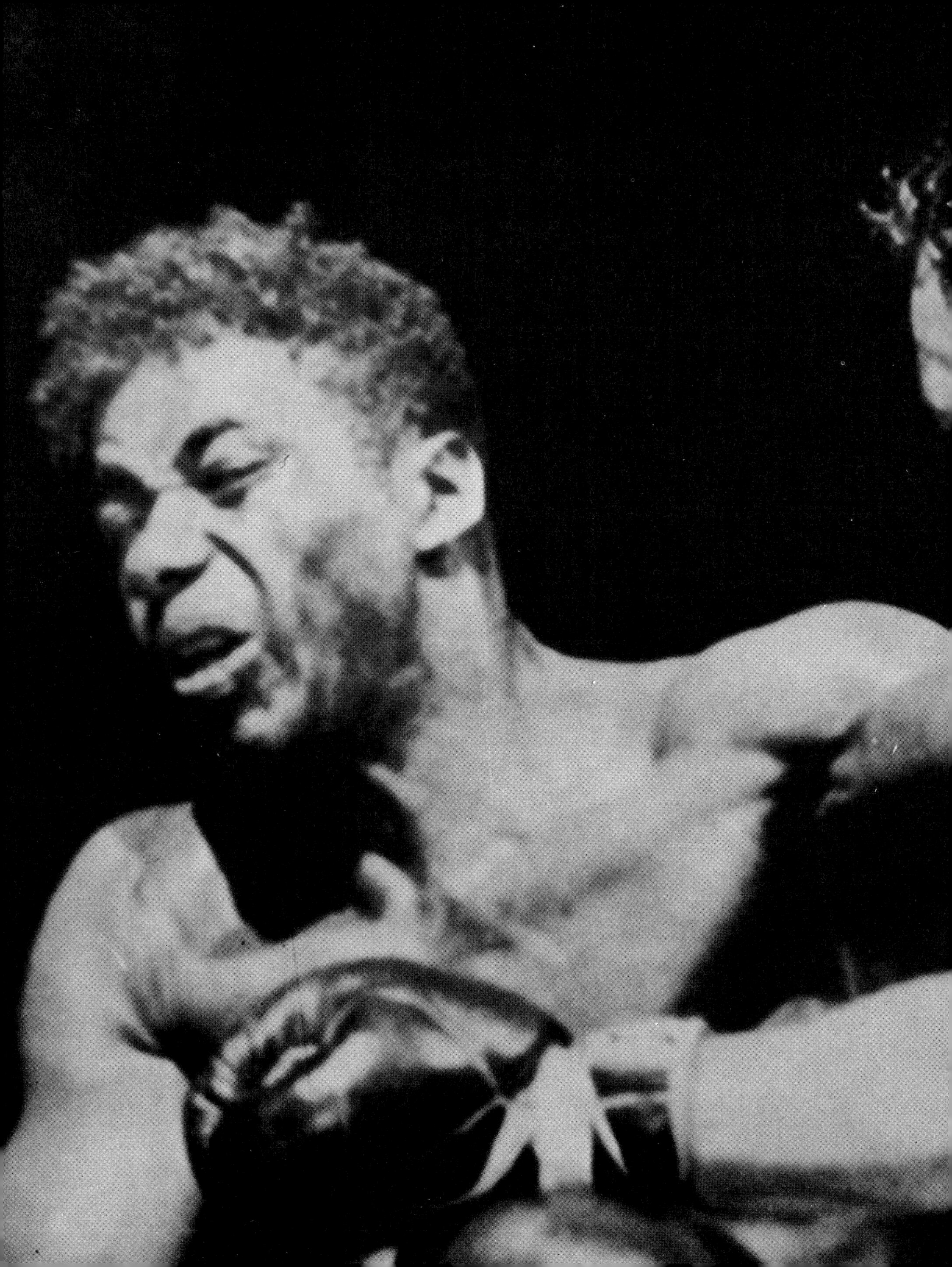

EVER

Previous pages
Brian London's greatest moment. In Indianapolis, 1959, he rocks world heavyweight champion Floyd Patterson in the third round. But Brian, from Blackpool, could not make it stick. He lost in the 11th.

missing from his right hand, the result of a factory accident in 1956. Yet Winstone took part in five world title fights.

The first three were against the hard Mexican, Vicente Saldivar, and Winstone was beaten each time, although the points decision against him in the second fight in Cardiff was debatable. The Welshman could have been forgiven for thinking he would never be world champion. But in 1968, after considerable political manoeuvring, he was able to fight the Japanese, Mitsunori Seki, in London. He won – not the undisputed world title, but at least one version of it. What might he have achieved with a complete fistful of fingers?

Dave Charnley, a chunky lightweight of Scots descent from Dartford, Kent, was for years described in the papers as 'Britain's finest fighter, pound for pound'. It was undoubtedly true. He was unlucky to have been at his peak at the time when Joe Brown, of New Orleans, was the world champion. Brown, known as 'Old Bones', was already 33 when Charnley fought him the first time in Houston, Texas. Charnley was stopped with a badly cut eye. Sixteen months later they met again, at Earls Court, London. Like the 18,000 other spectators, I thought Charnley had won, but referee Tommy Little decided otherwise and left the ringside under police escort. Two years later, in 1963, Charnley knocked out the now-ancient Brown in six rounds at Manchester, but by then 'Old Bones' no longer held the world title.

Alan Rudkin, of Liverpool, was a member of the famous Great Britain amateur side that whitewashed the USA 10–0 at Wembley in 1961. As a professional, he combined skill and two-fisted power. He deserved to be world champion and had three tries, against different opponents, each time on their territory, many thousands of miles from home. The opponents were all first-class world champions: Masahiko Harada, of Japan, with whom he went 15 rounds in Tokyo; Lionel Rose, the Australian Aborigine, whom he just failed to beat in Melbourne, and Ruben Olivares, the hard-bitten Mexican who destroyed Alan in Los Angeles. Rudkin's pro career spanned 10 years and when he retired in 1972 he was still the British and Commonwealth champion.

Perhaps the greatest near-miss suffered in my time as a reporter happened to Terry Downes, our former world middleweight champion, who at Belle Vue, Manchester, 1964, seemed certain to win the world light-heavyweight title from Willie Pastrano, of New Orleans, a light-hitting but delightfully clever boxer. On this night Pastrano seemed lethargic and lacking in willpower. Downes was all over him. Pastrano, however, had one supreme asset: a man called Angelo Dundee, working in his corner. Dundee, the genius who

The shot that tells you everything about the ferocious fighting Freddie Mills. The right is obviously cocked. Seconds later, he knocks the veteran Len Harvey out of the ring, and out of boxing. This was 1942, wartime, at Spurs football ground. After the war, Freddie won the world light-heavyweight title. Yet Harvey, a peerless boxer, was never able to do that.

Ernie Roderick (right), a master boxer from Liverpool, faces the American Henry Armstrong at Harringay in 1939, with the world welterweight title at stake. Roderick went the full 15 rounds, but Armstrong, the only man to hold three world titles simultaneously, was too busy for him.

Howard Winstone (right), the best featherweight to come out of Wales since Jim Driscoll, had three goes at taking the world title from tough Mexican, Vicente Saldivar, but was beaten each time. This was his first attempt, at Earl's Court, London, in 1965.

On the left, one of the best British fighters I ever saw; lightweight Dave Charnley. This is his world title fight in London with America's Joe Brown. I thought southpaw Charnley won, but the decision went to 'Old Bones' Brown, a great modern negro champion. The referee needed a police escort.

guided Muhammad Ali throughout his career, knew better than any of us how close Pastrano was to defeat. When they came out for the 11th, Dundee rounded off the vehement verbal lashing he had been giving Pastrano by whacking the American across the seat of his pants and yelling at him: 'Get out there, Daddy-O, and get going!'

Angelo had done the same thing to Ali only months before in Miami, in the world title fight with Sonny Liston. It had worked then, and it worked now. The transformation in Pastrano was incredible. He was no longer lethargic, but lethal. As Downes moved in confidently to attack once more, Pastrano side-stepped and swung a simple left-right. Downes, taken totally by surprise, was down, dazed, for 'eight'. When he got up, Pastrano

Liverpool's brilliant Alan Rudkin forces Masahiko 'Fighting' Harada to cover up in Tokyo. Harada kept his world bantam title, on points. Alan flew thousands of miles in three attempts on the title. Each time he came up against exceptional champions and never won the crown he deserved.

A rare sight: Terry Downes on the floor, with American Willie Pastrano trying not to trip over him. At Belle Vue, Manchester, in 1964, irrepressible Cockney Downes came within an ace of taking Willie's world light-heavyweight title. But manager Angelo Dundee 'psyched' Willie into an 11th-round victory.

dropped him again, and the referee stopped it, there and then. We all thought it hasty at the time, but, on reflection, Andrew Smyth probably saved Downes from worse damage. That second world title, however, had escaped Terry for ever.

The disappointment of the boxer who gets his big chance and sees it slip away is profound. There are some lines written by Lord Tennyson in his epic 'In Memoriam' which make the point:

Be near me when my light is low,
When the blood creeps, and the nerves prick
And tingle; and the heart is sick,
And all the wheels of Being slow.

Strangely enough, in that same poem Tennyson wrote:
He seems so near and yet so far.

Overpage
The picture that speaks for all those who come so near, and yet . . . Don Cockell (right) tries to fend off yet another Rocky Marciano assault. He can't. He knows that defeat is just a question of time. The chance of a lifetime has come . . . and gone.

BENLEE
BENLEE
BENLEE
BENLEE

CHAPTER TEN
THE WINNER

The winner has his gloves yanked off and stands, grinning, centre-ring, bandaged hands lifted high above his head, turning this way and that as photographers yell. His handlers stand either side, where some of the publicity may wash over them. If they come from a camp that rarely makes champions, they will be grinning hugely too. If the camp is used to winners, they may not smile at all. There have been champions in the past and there will be champions in the future. Let's get the pictures took and get to hell out of here.

The winner is courted by the man from the Board, all smiles and dinner-suit, carrying the Belt. A handshake, a trite word or two and the Belt is snapped fast round the sweaty body. More pictures.

The winner is courted by the man from radio or TV, all smiles and rumpled clothes, carrying the mike. The interview is sketchy, predictable and totally unheard by the crowd, who get restless. The manager is restless, too, unless he's been worked into the interview. Euphoria wanes, because the crowd are temporarily locked out of the celebrations.

The winner hoists his fists once more, bows awkwardly to all four sides of the ring and the cheers come again. Friends and relations, the ones who weren't saucy enough to invade the ring, fidget impatiently at the foot of the steps. He's theirs. They can't wait to get at him. Helmeted police, the only impassive people in the place, also wait. Up in the ring, a foot presses down the bottom rope and a hand lifts the middle rope, to stretch an exit for the winner. Escorted by police, he leads a crazy conga line back through the ranks of yelling people and waving flags. The procession floods over and past the next pair of boxers coming in.

The winner is worked through the jam of chattering reporters at the dressing-room door and shoved inside. The handlers get inside. Some friends and relations, the forceful ones, slip inside. The door is forced back against the mob and locked. Police mount guard and reporters wear out their knuckles rapping the woodwork. Voices are raised in unheeded complaints about the rights of the Press.

The winner hugs his mates, sips tea, looks at himself in the mirror to assess damage, flops on the couch, wipes sweat from his face again and again with the towel round his neck, swears joyously over his prospects and agrees with everything that everybody says. The hammering on the door is non-stop. When the lock is turned, the Press come tumbling in with notebooks and tape-recorders. The last few can barely force themselves in, so great is the crush. Questions, the same old, old questions, are flung. Did you think you had him going early on? Were you surprised when he went down? Did he hurt you? Was it easier than you expected? Did the right hand stand up OK? What was that your manager said to you before the last round? What are your plans now? Will you give him a return?

The winner showers, dresses and leaves. The night's fights are over, but well-wishers hang around for a glimpse of him. He is sore and tired, but doesn't care. He's off to the late-night celebration booked beforehand. He gets to bed at 3am and cannot sleep.

The winner buys a new home, his wife a fur coat. He makes his parents comfortable. He buys new suits for the new life that's hit him. Semi-respectable businessmen make dubious offers—'With your name on it, how can we go wrong?' He is recognized in the street. He is welcome at charity lunches, sportsmen's dinners, Awards of the Year, supermarket openings, television quizzes and *Desert Island Discs*. His hand is pumped, his back slapped, his ego flattered.

The winner's OK . . . until the day he becomes a loser.

CHAPTER ELEVEN
THE LOSER

The loser leaves the ring swiftly, unnoticed except by the disgruntled patron in the front row who did his money on him and who swears a silent obscenity as he goes by.

The loser walks hurriedly back to the sheltering anonymity of the dressing-room. He can't retreat fast enough from the scene of the other man's triumph and his own humiliation. His handlers are set-faced, stonily silent, trudging along behind him. Sympathizers in the crowd, with their well-meaning commiseration, get short shrift on the lonely march back.

The loser has no difficulty getting into his dressing-room. No-one is clamouring at the door. It slams shut behind him.

The loser is confused in the darkness of defeat. The manager's halting exposition makes it worse . . . if only you . . . perhaps we should have . . . that knockdown . . . he threw a lucky punch . . . the guy was dead tired . . . lucky bastard . . . we'll get him again . . . it'll be different next time. The words are futile, pointless.

The loser is crying. He worked his guts out for this chance. Never trained harder. Felt great. He told his mates he'd win for sure. They came along to share in it. Where are they now? One or two, genuinely sorry for him, are quietly knocking at the door. The rest? Drowning their pretended sorrows and assuring one another he'd never really been in with a chance, anyway.

The loser is sore and tired and feels it. He had a celebration booked beforehand. They can forget that. There is nowhere to go but home. A reporter comes in, looking for a quote, and makes the mistake of telling him what a game loser he was. Game loser? Who wants to be remembered as a game loser? Get out, you berk. Only he doesn't say it. Just thinks it.

This loser is never going to be champion, not rich, flattered, feted, clapped or courted. He showers, dresses and leaves. The night's fights are still going on. No one is waiting to wish him well. He goes to bed at midnight and cannot sleep. He lies there, wishing he were 12 years old again, starting out. He wishes he were full of hope and starry-eyed ambition, instead of staring 40 years' obscurity in the face.

Losers know all about The Hardest Game.

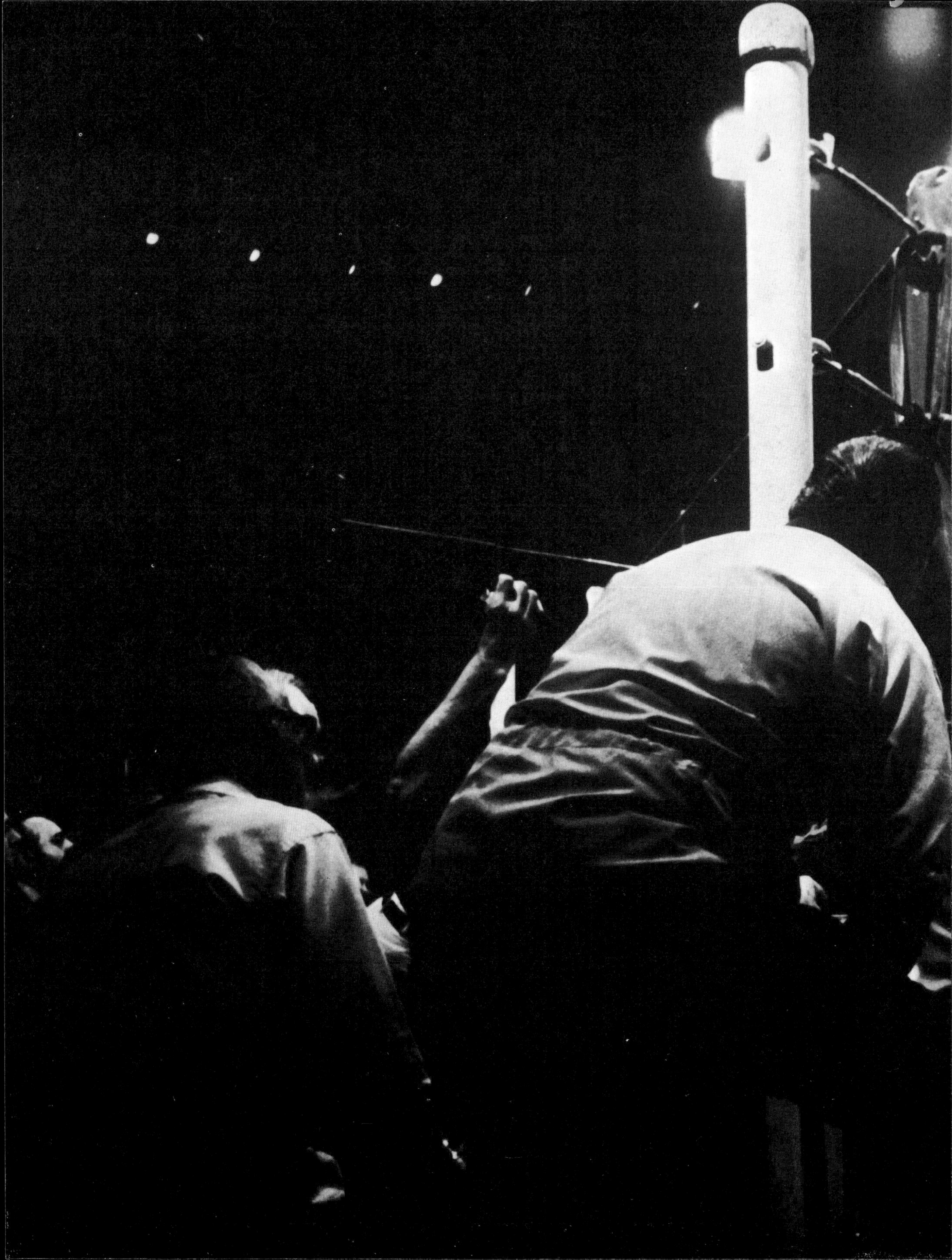